Art's
Principles

WILSON
LAFFERTY

Art's Principles

50 years
of hard-learned
lessons in building
a world-class
professional
services firm

Arthur Gensler
with Michael Lindenmayer

Written by Arthur Gensler with Michael Lindenmayer
Illustrations by Doug Wittnebel

First Printing: March 2015
Wilson Lafferty

www.artsprinciples.com

ISBN-13 978-0-9861069-0-3
ISBN-13 978-0-9861069-1-0

"This book is a pithy, pragmatic compilation of the uniquely personal ideas that have powered Art Gensler's leadership in building his remarkable firm."

— TED W. HALL

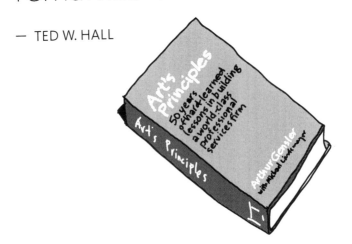

Foreword

Art Gensler's leadership role in architecture and design is
equivalent to Marvin Bower (McKinsey & Company) in
consulting, David Ogilvy (Ogilvy & Mather) in advertising,
or Henry Kravis (KKR) in private equity. Each of these
men established, some would say invented, professional
services firms in arenas where there were no precedents.
Each created an approach to managing a complex firm
that provided a new professional service of extraordi-
narily high quality to the leading companies in the world.
Just as significantly, Art established a true professional
services firm, one that is now self-governed and self-
perpetuating, in the arena of architecture and design.
Before Gensler, egocentric individual practitioners dom-
inated in a plethora of small firms.

The remarkable scale and geographic scope of the
Gensler architecture firm, now the world's largest, is a
mystery to most people in the design world. How could
a design firm withstand the centrifugal force generated
by an organization of 4,800+ highly talented designers

and architects who are spread over 46 offices on six continents? Even more mysterious, scratch any one of these professionals, and the talk will almost instantaneously turn to an odd mantra about a "one-firm firm."

The mystery of the Gensler success looms so large because the typical organizational approach in a design firm has been "one man, one castle," with only one strong ego dominating an almost feudal organizational form. Firms often are embroiled in internally focused battles over issues of status, recognition, and compensation. Once a new prince emerges, the typical outcome is a battle royal, followed by one or more of the protagonists leaving to start a new firm.

In contrast, Art built an enduring firm that accommodates many strong wills operating in a framework of "one firm." Many marvel and wonder, "How did he do this?"

This book, *Art's Principles*, is a pithy, pragmatic compilation of the uniquely personal ideas that have powered Art Gensler's leadership in building his remarkable firm. Do not expect sophisticated interlocking theories of organization or a treatise on the behavioral idiosyncrasies of design professionals. Rather, you will find a rich array of common sense approaches to managing a firm, a team, and one's own work.

These ideas are unified by Art's self-confident commitment to ensuring the success of others—which in turn ensures the success of the greater firm. Primary in this commitment to others is "client first," which is also the essential mantra of the most successful professional services firms in every field. Art built a large-scale firm that focused the organization's energy on serving clients, as opposed to who was winning the internal game of "king of the castle."

Art's Principles will enrich the understanding of effective leadership for anyone trying to lead—or "herd cats"—in a professional services firm. His ideas are broadly applicable, and have endured the heat generated in a crucible fired by high, creative energy. All professional services firms have strong, highly talented individuals with deep, narrow expertise, who vigorously express their very strong—typically self-centered—opinions. But, these kinds of pressures are especially high among design practitioners. Few design professionals innately understand the issues of managing a professional services firm. Many are artists (or think they are) who have deep-seated distain for structure and managing. As a result, Art's ideas have probably been tested more vigorously (and realistically) than any peer-reviewed journal on management could achieve. Not surprisingly, Art's well-tested ideas are reliably applicable to any professional services firm.

Art's Principles is easily accessible. You can drop into this book at almost any spot and receive a quick dose of pragmatic sustenance. Read all of it and you will access wisdom gained over 50 remarkable years. Whether you are leading a professional services firm or just getting started in your career, you will want to keep this book nearby on the nightstand.

TED W. HALL
Director Emeritus, McKinsey & Company
January 11, 2015

Preface

Architect Turned Entrepreneur

I always wanted to be an architect. When I was six years old, I would draw house floor plans and build models. I constructed buildings with my Lincoln Logs and erector sets. Legos had not yet been invented.

A few years after I started our company, it became obvious that I needed to know more than how to design and construct a building. It was essential that I learn how to be an entrepreneur and run a business.

Today, Gensler is the largest architectural design firm in the world, with 4,800 professionals in 46 offices in 14 countries. People often ask me whether I knew that I would create such a large firm. Definitely not! My original dream was to have about a six-person firm to design houses and perhaps some small buildings. The reality is beyond anything I ever dreamed.

These are basic
principles of business
that make a professional
services firm great.

How It All Began

I grew up during the Second World War. Because my dad was too old to be drafted, he stayed home and ran the New England office for a building materials company. I remember visiting a few architects' offices with him during that time and thinking this was the career for me. I had no idea what that meant.

My dad, who was a great salesman, coached me early in life. I put his advice to work doing door-to-door sales of magazine subscriptions until I had earned enough money to buy a good baseball glove.

Passion for Sportsmanship

I am a believer in good sportsmanship. It taught me how to handle myself both in business and in life. The Soap Box Derby, a popular nationwide competition, sparked my enthusiasm at an early age. The Derby had everything I loved: design, hard work, and competition. Participants had to invest in a starter kit of four wheels and a steering wheel. After that, it took $5 (the maximum you could spend) and one's imagination—and no help from parents.

Fortunately for me, my dad had a basement workshop. During the winter after basketball practice, I spent my afternoons and evenings diligently building my car. I finally allowed Dad to see my work. He took one look and said, "Son, that car will not win anything, so you better start over."

Discouraged but determined, I followed his advice and completely rebuilt that car. I'm proud to admit Dad was right—I ultimately took first place in the 11- and 12-year-old category. Although I lost in the finals against the 13- and 14-year-olds, I realized then that the disappointment of losing was not as great as the joy of winning.

Taking the Plunge

Fast forward to 1965. With $200 to my name, my wife handling administrative functions, our one draftsman Jim Follett, and a major contract in tow, we founded the Gensler firm. We were fortunate that my parents had gifted us $10,000 as a down payment on our first house.

Little did I know what lay ahead, or some of the major decisions we would have to make as we hired more staff. Step by step, we added offices. We became a national and then a global firm. During all this time, we continued to add services and products.

Our Tough Decisions along the Way

- To open New York City, Chicago, and Boston offices when we were warned that we must cooperate with certain individuals or we could not enter those markets. We refused to bend to those threats, and have been very successful without their participation.

- To form an in-company management committee of young leaders, bypassing some of our best professionals with more seniority at the risk of losing them. We did not.

- To not set up offices or profit centers with bonus pools by office because we felt it would limit firm-wide collaboration (see also Chapter 43, *No Silos*).

- To open our first overseas office with our own people in London where the laws, procedures, and processes were vastly more difficult than those we encountered in the United States.

- To work in the Middle East and China, where many US architectural firms had experienced enormous difficulties, especially in getting paid and being dealt with fairly.

We had no roadmaps. Over time, we developed a core set of principles that have worked. We often learned by trial and error.

The Service Professionals' Blind Spot

Do you dream of running your own business one day or growing the one where you work?

Many service professionals share your dream of the independence and financial freedom that come with building one's own business. However, I have observed that most service professionals suffer from a major blind spot: they invest heavily to become great technicians, but they have little knowledge about business.

Without understanding basic business principles, it is nearly impossible to fulfill your dreams. We propose in this book to help remove the blind spot that is holding you back from succeeding.

Start from the Beginning

The earlier you learn business skills, the better. It is important that universities and business schools integrate these skills into their programs. Without incorporating them into their business curricula, schools will produce students who struggle to fulfill their dreams.

Even if students and professionals have zero ambition of running their own firms, their understanding of how business works will help them be better team members and ensure their ability to develop successful careers.

Going on Your Own

I believe it is never too late to pursue your dream. You might be a senior manager looking to build your own venture, or you might be looking to remain engaged, stay active, and, ultimately, become a leader in your current organization.

If you are serious about pursuing your dream, invest in understanding the basic principles of business that make a professional services firm great. You will develop the confidence required to make that leap toward success.

I hope the principles described in this book will help you develop yourself, your team, and your organization.

ARTHUR GENSLER
March 2015

Introduction

This book is meant for service professionals to gain insights that can help them become better at business. Our principles show a pathway to building a successful firm or growing in a firm where you are employed.

Service Professionals

While I come from the design and architecture world, this book is open to anyone who has gained a professional technical skill. This includes accountants, attorneys, and management consultants. It includes doctors, interior designers, engineers, and architects. You could be a graphic or industrial designer. You might be a financial service advisor.

This book is for you.

Common Ground

Three characteristics are common across these diverse professional fields:

- First, the firms operating in these worlds rely on people for their value creation.

- Second, these people invest an enormous amount of effort, time, and financial resources to become excellent technical professionals.

- Third, while most of these individuals focus on becoming the best technical experts in their field, they often miss out on acquiring the business skills necessary to be successful in the marketplace.

You need to understand the basic business skills of running a professional services firm, whether you are an employee, manager, or entrepreneur. Good business skills enable you to communicate your value, win business, and obtain opportunities to improve the lives of your clients.

Good business is for everyone.

The Big Ideas

Four Big Ideas underlie the principles in this book: Family, Sharing, Trust, and Adding Value.

- Firm as Family is a unifying concept that brings together many of the principles.

- The importance of Sharing: although "eat what you kill" may be an accepted norm, you shouldn't do it that way. Instead, institutionalizing the Monday Morning Call reinforces the concept of sharing.

- Putting all dealings into the context of Building Trust, internally and with clients, is a concept that business literature rarely discusses but is key to success.

- Adding Value is incredibly important. Providing only standard service will not create an organization of excellence.

Nontechnical Introduction

I am sharing principles I picked up through decades
of hard-learned lessons while building a service firm.
I had zero formal training in business. I wrote this book
because it is one I wish had existed when I ventured out
to start my own firm. This book is meant to help guide
you and whet your appetite to pick up more business
skills, which are vital to building a thriving life.

If you are a service professional and want to succeed,
then leverage the Four Big Ideas. To maximize the
principles covered in this book, you don't need to start
at the beginning and work your way through to the end.
Find a topic that interests you and get started.

Become passionate about the opportunity. Once
you develop your approach to the various principles
discussed, you will be able to pursue your dreams and
achieve your goals.

Enjoy!

Building Service Companies

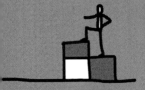

Common Sense Principles

A Common Sense Approach

It can take years for service professionals to gain and master technical skills—a commitment that requires both time and money. This upfront investment often makes service professionals delay acquiring business skills because they think it will take too much time and effort.

The good news is that basic business skills can be acquired quickly if you use a common sense approach. I'm a champion of keeping things simple, getting rid of unnecessary jargon, and applying principles that work over time.

Time-Tested Principles

I will not explain how to be the best accountant, how to make detailed strategic plans, or tell you which legal forms to fill out. Instead, I offer you time-tested principles based on the lessons I have learned over the course

You know when it's right.
But why does it take so
long to get there?

of running a business that has been profitable for 50 consecutive years.

All kinds of management fads come and go. I have experimented with most of them or watched others try them out in their firms. Over the decades, I have relied on the best lessons from my own experience or those gained by others.

Adjust and Adapt

While these principles apply to most service firms, it is important that you draw from your own experience and adjust and adapt these principles to fit your situation. This book is meant to be a starting point to help you establish the foundation of your business skills.

My hope is that you build on this foundation, and that you try to always learn from those around you and from other professionals whom you respect.

Reaching Scale

Size Selection

Businesses come in various sizes, from sole practitioners to global enterprises. Your task is to determine the size of the firm that works best for you and your associates.

I respect any firm that has figured out how to create value and meet clients' needs. Successful firms can be small or large, but **it is essential that they all begin small**. First, ask yourself the key question: How big do you want to grow your firm? Once you answer that, you need to understand the steps required to reach the scale best for your business.

"The bottom-line question is: Precisely what is it that you want to be famous for?"

— TOM PETERS

Growing Possibilities and Responsibilities

Growing a firm and reaching scale will continually open up new possibilities. With scale come the opportunities to explore new geographies, to develop new practice areas, and to enhance skills. Scale also brings more of everything: more responsibilities and complexities, more clients and employees, and fresh risks to understand and manage. You must be committed to grasping and acting on these at each stage of your firm's growth, thereby constantly evolving your organization.

Scaling Service Companies

Moving slow and steady is fundamental in scaling service companies because they rely on human talent. It takes time to find talent, to groom and generate value, just as it takes time to win clients and build a book of business. You must earn trust while you customize value per client. Accordingly, repeat client work relies on that client's success at growing their own book of business.

Service companies differ from product companies or Internet ventures. Products are about mass production. Internet ventures reach millions of subscribers in a relatively short time in the online world, with technology doing much of the work. On the other hand, service companies, whose operations rely deeply on people, must work day after day to win each and every client. If you want to reach scale in a service firm, you must keep the long view in mind.

New Skills, Same Principles
While scaling requires new skills at every stage of growth, one thing remains constant: the set of principles that serves as the foundation for your growth. I am sharing those principles that can help any service firm reach the scale that best suits them.

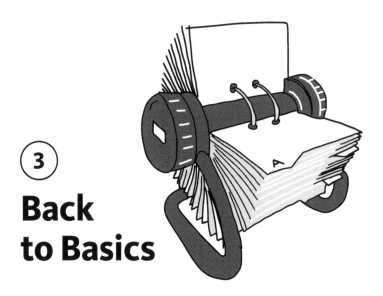

3

Back
to Basics

To build a great firm, you must master the basics of running a business. This set of principles covers the basics that every service firm needs in order to grow.

Talent
The starting point for every service firm is its people. Of necessity, you must find, train, and deploy the best talent to serve your clients' needs. To get this right, you need to develop a strong culture that encourages your talent to do their best work and to be passionate about your firm. The bigger you grow, the more complex the

management is. As you gain size, you need to develop your firm's leadership abilities. Your employees are not robots. What a family does to ensure that each member thrives, you must do for your employees in and out of the workplace.

Running the Business

The three main things you must execute well are strategy, sales, and implementation. With the right strategy, you know the client you are serving and what you are offering. Because sales are your firm's lifeblood, you must have paying clients to sustain the business. They are what fuel your ability to do great work, put food on your table, and send your kids to college. Without sales, you go bust. Finally, to earn client respect and repeat business, you must learn how to be productive and efficient in your implementation.

Daily Improvement

Building a great firm is not achieved by one super-heroic act. Instead, every day you must focus on being better. By concentrating on daily improvements to your business practices, you will be able to keep ahead of your competition and do your best work.

Commitment to Excellence
Let's face it—to be great takes commitment. You will find no easy way to avoid it. While you will be able to quickly absorb the basic principles of growing a business, you will spend years of hard work in the pursuit of excellence to master these skills and to spread them throughout your firm.

Repeat it over & over again.

Continuous Learning

As you build your business, you will face many challenges. Use this book and a wide range of other sources as guides to strengthen your business abilities. Embrace and commit to continuous learning. It is the only way to keep up with the rate of change that impacts every service sector.

Over and Over Again

Once I discover a technique that works well, I use it over and over again. I also repeatedly drill it into my team. Never assume that doing something once or sharing an insight once will be enough. It is not. It is the daily repetition of what works that becomes a positive habit and eventually part of your core culture. If you find that the times have changed and that what once worked no longer applies, you must actively figure out what does work and then get the message out to your team.

As a firm, we decided we would not work on health-care projects. Many firms have in-depth experience in hospitals, and although it is one of the largest practice areas for architects, it was not what we wanted to do. But after many years of saying "no," a number of our people felt there was a viable niche in "wellness" where our experts could add value. We now have a new practice area.

If you build a learning organization, your team will welcome change. However, for the change to persist, every day you need to repeat the new lesson learned. That is how improvement gradually builds into a sustained edge on your competition and makes your organization a place where the best and brightest want to work.

Culture

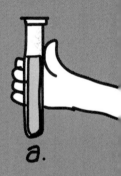

a.

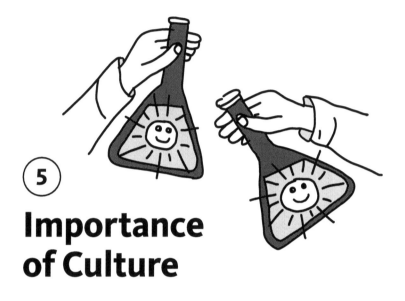

5

Importance of Culture

From the beginning, build a culture in your firm. While this culture will evolve as you move from a small start-up to a fully functioning firm, your core values will take root and remain the same over time. To change culture, not to mention current management practices, is difficult.

Many kinds of cultures exist. Culture is strategic. You could have a military-style organization with all the power concentrated in the hands of a few, with a clear chain of command. Or you could opt for a totally decentralized organization with limited formality. However, the one I encourage is a **family culture**, because I think it is the most enduring and most successful over time.

Mindset vs. Manuals
Most people think that culture is what is printed in the human resources manuals that everyone must follow upon joining your firm. Culture is not about manuals. It is about setting behavior and style. Culture relates to how your team treats clients and each other. It is about how they tackle problems and create value. It concerns the presence of guiding principles that help your people be their best both at work and at home. Culture is a leadership tool.

The sum total of how people apply your guiding principles and act on this mindset is your firm's culture. You will see that strong culture leads to strong performance.

Live It
A strong culture develops when everyone from the front-desk staff to the founder lives by the guiding principles. It is what people do when management isn't looking. Your firm's culture endures when people live the values consistently. A strong culture helps attract and retain both the best talent and clients, because they recognize the level of excellence that guides you. Accept it and contribute to it.

Build an enduring family culture.

Repeat It

Setting a behavior requires two things: a clear set of values and a relentless willingness to constantly repeat the message of those values. Use all means of internal and external communication to get your message across so that it is clear to your team and clients what you represent in the marketplace.

Mergers of Firms

Let me caution you about a merger of your firm or purchase of another firm to help you grow a new service or expand to a new location. Most mergers present a threat to a firm's culture—both yours and theirs. Changing the name on the door does not promote compatibility, nor does it mean that the two cultures are easily combined into one enhanced culture. Establishing your family beliefs takes a long time, and unless you are prepared to work diligently on the integrity of the two organizations, you should avoid mergers.

Be a Family

Families Stick Together

While it might seem unfashionable in today's culture, I am still a fan of building a family mindset at work. Strong families celebrate the good times and find their way through the tough ones. It is not always easy, but in the end, it is worth it. You work together and play together.

No-Jerk Rule

Family means thinking about more than yourself. It means finding fresh opportunities for others, supporting them as they figure out something difficult, and being aware of how others feel. Accordingly, if I observe someone who is selfish and acting like a jerk, I will invite them to leave, despite any great talent they might have. That type is toxic, and you should never let your firm be a dumping ground for such behavior. Fortunately for me, these situations have been very infrequent because of the care and time we take in our hiring process. If you want a healthy, family-firm spirit, make sure you have a "no-jerks policy" in place.

We vs. I

Family is about the power of "We." Take note of how often you start a sentence with I: "I did this" and "I did that." Research at the University of Texas suggests that people who lead with "I" sentences are less powerful and less sure of themselves. In other words, families are stronger than individuals. Start with "We."

Have Fun

Family means bonding time. Yet during tough times at most firms, it's the company parties, company-sponsored sports leagues, and leadership meetings that tend to be eliminated first. Rethink your plans before cutting any one of these. You can always redesign them with fewer frills, but getting rid of these events means you lose the quality time necessary for your team to be together outside the workplace.

It's a good idea to offer events that are pure fun as well. We have done our best over the years to plan activities where shoptalk is left in the office. We want our people exchanging views, inspiring ideas in each other, and building trust through fun experiences. I believe there is life after 6:00 p.m. Have one!

Money Where Your Mouth Is

Family is a deep level of commitment. One way to deepen it further is to make sure that your interests are aligned. We do this with an Employee Stock Ownership Program (ESOP). From the front desk to the CEO, everyone has a chance to participate and align their interests with the family. I relate an ESOP to the difference between a homeowner and a renter. If you own your home, you have a stake in it and constantly strive to maintain it and improve it. If you are a renter, you simply live there. Similarly, ownership (e.g., an ESOP) encourages your team to improve themselves and their firm. People thought I was crazy when I first gave out my stock, but if you want a family culture, everyone must be in it together. In the end, the remaining stock I have has become far more valuable than if I had kept it all for myself.

Take a Look:

Share the
Financial Health

Each year we hold a principals' meeting in a city where
we have an office. We invite spouses and significant
others to attend all our meetings and events. It's
an opportunity to get to know each other better, to
share insights, and for the local office to showcase its
city. We attempt to spark new thoughts and inspiration by inviting prominent speakers to our gatherings.

While it is important for everyone to build strong
relationships, we also want the employees and their
families to have a clear view of our financial health as
an organization. At our annual meeting, we dedicate
a session to our financials. We feel this approach is
key to having a strong family culture inside and outside of the office.

One-Firm Firm

Be a One-Firm Firm

Most professional services firms are small. Those that figure out how to expand up to 50 employees often stall out and are unable to reach scale beyond that point. One of the main reasons they struggle is that they fail to develop a one-firm firm mindset and a family culture. You need the culture to go with the mindset of full sharing and teamwork.

Hire the Best Advisors

As we started to grow and expand our practice areas geographically, we decided to look for organizations that could be role models. All of the organizations we observed in our type of business lived by rules very unlike the ones we wanted for our firm. They had different cultures. Instead, we searched for a management consulting firm and found McKinsey & Company. While working with them, we developed our "one-firm firm" philosophy. The building block of our business would be

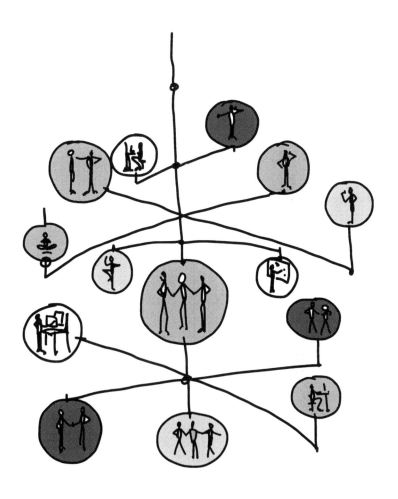

a studio versus an office location. We also established our "constellation of stars" approach rather than a "single star" mindset.

As you work to determine what is best for your firm, consider bringing in wise experts. The time we spent with David Maister, an expert in running professional services firms, was invaluable. Whether you have a management consulting, accounting, or legal firm, hire the best. It will pay back in great dividends.

Single Star Systems

Most small or medium-sized professional services firms emerge on the efforts of a single, star player. That individual might be a highly regarded service professional, such as an attorney, designer, or management consultant. Clients will recognize this person's talent and want to make sure that the star of the firm is intimately involved in all aspects of their specific project. Their attitude is that everyone else is simply background and support. This caps what is possible because a single star has only a limited time available in a day. I believe there is a different way forward that helps small firms slowly grow larger. This is the one-firm firm model.

A Constellation of Stars

Instead of building your firm on the power of a single star, I suggest you build a constellation of stars. Attract top talent throughout your organization, from the receptionist to your executive office to your back-office functions.

The constellation model is important for three reasons:

- First, clients get much better value and service. A depth of talent in a constellation of stars exists no matter how bright the single star seems to shine.

- Second, the process of working with your entire organization is a quality experience for your client. This removes the friction of doing business with you. The easier it is to contract with you, the more repeat work you are likely to secure.

- Third, you build resiliency into your firm. A firm that relies on a single star is a high-risk venture. A constellation of stars is more likely to generate fresh ideas, stand strong during difficult times, and house an institutional memory that can help the firm grow from generation to generation.

Getting Stars to Work Together

Building a culture of collaboration, ownership, and fair sharing requires trust. In turn, trust requires honesty, candor, and an absence of self-interest. Before you hire or promote a professional, make sure they appreciate and live by these values of mutual support, which keep egos in check, eliminate silos, and are the glue that holds together highly talented people in a one-firm firm. For example, colleagues with these values will pitch in to help a fellow worker whose project is in trouble (see also Chapter 43, *No Silos*).

Give your team an opportunity to work and share the rewards together. You will need to build trust between them and the organization, but once they know the organization will treat them fairly, they will enjoy working together. Remember to keep internal politics out of your work. Internal politics do not belong in a business environment.

The Importance of

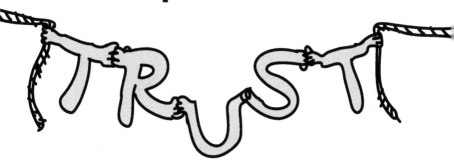

Powerful Currency

The most powerful currency of any relationship is trust. It is gained slowly and lost quickly. Once lost, it is nearly impossible to regain. Trust binds people together through good times and bad. You must gain a trusting relationship with your clients, business associates, and your employees. When people trust each other, they can deal with difficult situations, and they honestly celebrate each other's successes. You can be confident without being arrogant.

Invest in trust. It is always worth it.

It's always worth investing in trust.

Bad News and Change

Some situations drive people to avoid or disregard the truth. This can happen when things go wrong and a manager tries to cover up or gloss over the bad news—a terrible example of leadership. The correct approach if a project is proceeding in the wrong direction is to stop, face the problem, and figure out how to move in the right direction, even if it means having a difficult conversation with clients or employees. It is far better to deal with the pain and work through the challenge than to avoid the truth and compound the problem to the point where it cannot be resolved.

Change happens in life. Sometimes factors are out of your control and can impact your ability to deliver for a client. You will need to educate your client on the issue, find a work-around, and move forward. Holding out to the last minute to deliver the bad news or masking the issue will only cause serious damage to the relationship later.

Unchecked Ambition

Being ambitious is positive. Being greedy is not. Greed encourages lying. By grabbing a few extra dollars now, you lose the ability to build enduring relationships that are mutually beneficial over the long run. Greed shows up in big as well as small things, like expense reports. Greed destroys trust. Make sure to distinguish between ambition and greed.

The Benefits of Trust

Trust enjoys two major benefits. The first is with your clients. If they know you are honest and direct, they usually are willing to work through bad times, and they won't hesitate to be a referral source when things go well.

The second benefit is that authentic collaboration will take root within your firm. Employees will know that they can trust each other with their clients. They will naturally generate a strong internal referral market. They will also know that they can trust each other to fulfill their part of a project for a client.

These two benefits are the basis of a strong family culture and have served me well for five decades.

Take a Look:

Trust the Numbers

We were asked to propose design and planning services for a very large office campus. The project
consisted of multiple buildings and amenities features.
The client asked us to propose our approach and fee
for doing the work. I inquired about their project
budget. For whatever reason, they refused to give us
this information. When we made our presentation
and shared our fees with them, they were shocked
and said we were twice as high as another proposal.
I am pretty good with numbers and showed them how
I arrived at our fee. I felt quite comfortable that the
fee was where it ought to be.

However, they decided to accept the other proposal.
That firm was not local, but was staffed up to do the
project. After a few months, I read in the newspaper
that the client had stopped the project and was just
leasing space in an existing building. There was no
mention that the project had overshot its budget.

After that experience, the company returned to
us. They understood we were true to the numbers.
Today, we do all of their design and planning work.

Ethics

Always Be Ethical

There are no shortcuts when it comes to being ethical: either you are or you are not. It is the foundation of your character. It will stand the test of time, even if it means giving up a relationship if you cross paths with someone who is not ethical. If you lose a project due to another party's unethical practices, don't get mad, don't sue, don't complain, and don't lose sight of where you are headed. Another opportunity will arise.

Winners are ethical.

Be a Winner

Winners are ethical. They understand that being unethical might score some short-term gains, but that in the long run there are always consequences. Winners make their words count. When they make a promise, they keep it. By being ethical, winners make the whole business ecosystem stronger because people can trust one another.

Home and Abroad

Some cultures are poisoned by corruption. The key to your success is to stick to your standards. Do not ever lower them. It is a causal sequence that can put everyone at risk. It pays to always be ethical at home and abroad.

Take a Look:

No Laundering

We were doing a large interior project for the head of a major financial institution. One day he asked me to run some furniture for his house through our account. He was trying to have us launder the furniture purchases through the bank. I said, "No way." We ended our relationship. He ultimately ended up in jail; apparently somebody else decided this type of dealing was okay.

Fair Sharing

What Is Fair

Managing compensation is a difficult job. It is particularly challenging for first-time owners and new managers. They tend to either overpay or underpay. They try to please everyone or try to please only themselves. The key to eliminating the compensation challenge is to embrace fair sharing.

The Upside of Fair Sharing

There are five main upsides to fair sharing:

- You send a clear signal that your organization is a meritocracy, so everyone in your firm knows that their upward mobility is driven by their performance. They also realize that the results of their efforts are fairly rewarded. All too often, service firms turn into fiefdoms where people play favorites. Or worse, they become slave factories, where everyone works hard, and one person, or a few, eats up all of the profits.

- A family culture where everyone supports each other can take root. If you do not have a fair-sharing family culture, you are at risk of being a collection of mercenaries who fight and look out for themselves. They have no concern for the rest of the group.

- Collaboration can spread throughout your firm. If everyone knows that their contributions will be recognized and rewarded, they are much more likely to pitch in and help each other throughout the year to deliver superior results to clients.

- Everyone in your firm will concur with the long-term perspective. Our current marketplace is plagued by short-term vision: people trying to grab all that they can today while starving the organization's future growth. Short-term views are what fuel market bubbles that give us problems, such as the mortgage meltdown that devoured the global markets. When fair sharing exists, people want to stay with the firm. They want their company to exist and grow so that they can build a fruitful career.

• Finally, service firms often face an annual dilemma: they pay out all their cash and start with little left over to grow the firm into the new year. In a culture where fair sharing is embraced, your team will be willing to share in the investment it takes to grow the firm. They will understand it is important to retain a few dollars for growth or difficult times. Employees will accept a little less now so that the firm can get better and stronger. As a result of the strength of the firm, employees will be better positioned to build long-term personal wealth.

"Sharing means that a team has a common objective. As the saying goes: There are no winners on a losing team."

— MICHAEL HAMMER
Fortune magazine

Pooling the Profits

Many organizations distribute the money available for profit on a work unit or location basis. We believe that creates "silo thinking" and discourages sharing clients and information. We distribute profits on a firm-wide, value-delivered basis. Though more difficult to manage, it supports our one-firm firm culture of teamwork.

Stages of Sharing

Different ways of sharing exist at various stages of growth. When you are just starting out, I believe the easiest way to go about sharing is through a fair, basic salary with the possibility of a bonus. We build bonuses into our budget so that if we meet our budget, bonus money will be available for all.

Equity

Often start-ups will distribute equity to attract talent. I encourage caution on this because it takes time to figure out whether the new employee is a fit. If the fit fails, it is very difficult to buy back that equity. It's best to wait and make sure the individual matches your firm's culture.

Many firms require senior people to buy into the firm to obtain equity. While my family held all the equity when we started, we eventually opted to gift a portion of company stock in order to retain key individuals, therefore diluting our own equity percentage. Most of our people didn't have the cash to buy the stock, and I disliked the idea that they had to obtain a bank loan to purchase it. The commitment we received with this approach has been immense.

Profit Sharing

Distribution of profits is important. As a firm's profitably grows, setting up a formal profit-sharing scheme is the best route. A well-run profit-sharing plan can create great long-term value by providing resources for you and your people's retirement over many years. And again, when you reach scale and are thinking about how to grow the firm from generation to generation, I urge you to consider exploring an ESOP. This transforms every employee into an owner, and it provides a financially sound vehicle for ownership transition.

Leaders Are Last in Line

The clearest signal that your firm is fair sharing is when your leaders are last in line at bonus time. Your firm is likely to see good times with plenty to go around, and bad times with very little. Our policy was always to pay the leaders last, with me as the very last, when it was time to distribute the profits. We started with the back office and front desk, then worked our way up the ladder. In financially difficult times, there might not be anything to pay yourself as a leader. But when times are good, you are able to pay your leadership and yourself a healthy bonus.

When you apply this bonus policy to your firm, it goes a long way in demonstrating your commitment to your people. It shows that you put your team first. When you have a great year and you can pay yourself well, your team will be happy to see you, as an owner and manager and leader, thriving as well.

No Dirty Dishes

Pay Attention to Details

Determining your grand strategy is important in order to guide your business growth, but it is by paying attention to the small details that you become successful—including making sure there are no dirty dishes in the office kitchen sink.

No Dirty Dishes

From the beginning, it was my policy that everyone cleaned up after themselves and that throughout the day the kitchen sink was free of dirty dishes. Does this seem like an odd thing to worry about when you are fighting to stay alive as a start-up? Perhaps, but it is one of those small details that sends a signal to your team and to potential clients. It sends four key messages:

- You respect each other as teammates. It means you cared enough to give the next person a clean and clear space to go about their day.

- You must check your ego at the door when you come to work. No one is above doing dirty dishes. This attitude helps generate a culture where everyone pitches in and does whatever is needed to get the job done.

- It reinforces the start-to-finish mindset that I discuss in this book. Client work is full of dirty dishes. Some small detail always pops up in projects. Great service professionals roll up their sleeves and help figure out a solution for their clients.

- Every experience comes together to create what a potential or current client thinks about your brand. Your office is one big brand environment. You want your clients to know that you are a professional, respectful, and high-quality outfit.

A pile of dirty coffee mugs or a splattered microwave says just the opposite. Always make sure there are no dirty dishes!

Make It Fun

Life can be stressful. Of course, work life has all kinds of daily pressures. It is beneficial to recognize this and add some fun to your workplace.

Engaging Environment

As you can imagine, we care a great deal about making sure that people work in an engaging environment. What creates this kind of environment is specific to each profession and to each individual firm's culture.

The important thing is that you think about your environment. Engage your service professionals and see what they are seeking, both professionally and personally. Once you understand what they need and want, you can attempt to include it in the workplace.

Meaningful Work

Nothing kills the spirit faster than boring projects and a dead-end job feeling. If you want your team engaged and having fun, make sure they have meaningful work. Secure the kind of work that challenges them, improves their skills, and opens up their paths toward more challenging work.

Blow Off Some Steam

Understand that no matter what you do, life pressures will always be there. Sometimes a person needs to blow off some steam. Supporting sports teams and throwing proper parties are two ways to relieve pressure among your employees. Be sure that you attend and participate along with your people. These activities create a family culture and support the principle of sharing. If you are in a leadership position, be willing to expend more energy than expected to bring great energy to your team. It makes all the difference.

Party Planning Team

As your firm grows, include your team in the party planning. It helps confirm that you want to put together something they will enjoy, not just what you as the leader thinks they will enjoy. The planning and preparation are actually half the fun—an essential ingredient to keeping people smiling and content. A happy and healthy workplace is the foundation for a successful business.

Take a Look:

Big or Small,
Make an Effort

It does not matter if you are just starting out or are already a big firm. You need to make an effort. In the early days of our firm, we decided to throw a Christmas party for the children of our employees. We committed $15 for each child—a generous amount back then. I decided that we should have Santa hand out the gifts. Guess who picked up a simple suit and wore it to the party to hand out the gifts?

As we grew, the firm bought an elaborate Santa Claus suit. However, there was one problem. This suit was made for winter weather on Fifth Avenue in New York City. Our parties were on the West Coast and held indoors. So, this Santa felt like he was in a sauna, but the energy was amazing and that spirit carried forward into the new year.

Believe me, it was worth the effort. Figure out the best way to celebrate for your team.

Leadership

Key Attributes of a Leader

Attributes That Equal the Right Stuff

The world is a highly competitive place. Competition can fuel you to succeed or it can drive you out of business. Leadership and management are noble careers if done well. No other role offers so many ways to help others learn and grow. Strengthening your people and your teams brings gratification and reward. Your goal is to build a thriving and enduring business.

In building leadership teams with top-notch qualities, there are six main traits that you need to seek out and develop in your people.

DRIVE: It takes an incredible amount of initiative and energy to lead a team into the marketplace day after day and consistently win new business, deliver great value to clients, and keep ahead of your competitors.

Six main traits to
seek out and develop:
Drive
Integrity
Collaboration
Focus
Efficiency &
Effectiveness
Innovation

Drive must come from deep within a person. Driven individuals are passionate; they love to produce results, welcome more responsibility, and are marked by a strong will to win.

INTEGRITY: While there are many driven individuals who are hungry to win, it is essential that these people are equally committed to a life of integrity. This trait is also deeply ingrained in a person. It results in leaders who are direct, honest, and fair. People of integrity are in it for the long run. They understand that drive and ambition must be checked with integrity. They understand that it takes a long time to build trust, but only one bad decision to unravel it. Strong leaders figure out how to produce great results and sustain their integrity.

COLLABORATION: Some people think leadership means commanding and controlling others. While that may come with decision-making responsibility, it does not work well when you turn into a dictator. The best leaders are like great sports team coaches who express their role in the workplace through mentorship. Leaders understand that it takes a constant wave of young talent moving into leadership positions for a firm to expand into new services, geographies, and entirely new lines of business. Leaders see the firm as a family that wants their next generation to do well.

Your job as a leader is to be right at the end of the meeting, not at the beginning. It is your job to flush out the facts, all the opinions, and, in the end, make good decisions. You get evaluated on whether you made a good decision and not whether it was your idea from the beginning.

FOCUS: Focus is a rare attribute these days. With many gadgets, apps, and communities calling for your attention, it is easy to become busy, distracted, and unproductive. Strong leaders know how to concentrate their attention to keep their team's efforts focused on an endgame.

EFFICIENCY & EFFECTIVENESS: Leaders have the dual responsibilities of figuring out how to serve their clients efficiently and produce value. They also have the responsibility to do it in a cost-effective manner. One of the truths in business is that **if you don't start a project right, you can't finish it right**. We often get excited and want to start a project before we really know what the problem is.

Many talented service professionals are good at generating effective results, but they are unskilled at or disregard efficiency. As you recruit and build your leadership team, you need to groom people who demonstrate a commitment to efficiency and effectiveness with equal respect.

"The only sustainable competitive advantage comes from out-innovating the competition."

— JAMES MORSE

INNOVATION: While leaders need to focus on effectively and efficiently delivering on value to their clients today, they also need to spot oncoming trends. Competent leaders identify these oncoming trends and find ways to ready and position the firm to compete and avoid being blindsided by a disruptive competitor.

Work with your people when they get excited about a new idea. Support careful experimentation. Don't get caught up in "bet the farm" ideas, but explore innovation. Support it and embrace change when it is appropriate.

Innovation is key to catching new trends and delivering needed results. If you and your team are always looking forward toward how to best solve new challenges, you will have developed one of the key skills of leadership. Remember, what you measure gets done—to measure is to get results. People respond quickly if they see constant improvement when the outcomes are regularly measured.

Core Leadership Skills

Six Skills That Every Leader Needs

Being a great service professional does not necessarily make you a great leader. Most professional services firms struggle to identify, groom, and promote successful leaders. If you want to scale, you will need to be better than your competition at building a deep leadership bench. You need to seek out and develop the six skills that make for great leaders.

Six skills to seek out
and develop:
Focus
Decisiveness
Imagination
Commitment
Excellence
Communication

FOCUS: We all expect our top professionals to have the ability to concentrate on a single task until it is complete. While it is one thing to concentrate as an individual, it is another thing to have the skills required to get an entire team to focus and realize a mission. Skillful leaders are able to create an external focus that defines success in market terms. They are able to align talent and keep it on mission.

DECISIVENESS: Leaders make big and small decisions day after day. Some decisions will be easy, while others will be difficult. You need to be a leader or to appoint leaders who seek clarity and are confident decision-makers. All leaders must be accountable for their decisions.

IMAGINATION: Good leaders make good decisions. They must also have the skill to generate new possibilities. This might be fresh service ideas, new marketplaces to explore, or creative ways to do things more efficiently. Good leaders have imagination and the ability to spark it in their teams.

COMMITMENT: Leading a group of highly talented professionals is challenging. If you want to operate as more than a cluster of hired mercenaries, you need to inspire family spirit. The way to do that is to build commitment and loyalty. Individuals who lead by example do that successfully.

Avoid promoting people who use blame as an excuse or dominate the spotlight when there is a victory. These people will never be great leaders, even if they are technically gifted professionals. Do not tolerate individuals who are cynical or negative. They pit people against each other and expect others to work while they relax. People like this can destroy the foundation you've built for long-term success. Get rid of them.

EXCELLENCE: You want your leaders to develop excellence in either a function or market sector. Leaders consistently seek to improve their strengths, gain insights from others, and share their expertise with the team so that they can better serve clients and win new business.

COMMUNICATION: Plainspoken and direct is the style you want in a leader—someone who knows how to simplify complex ideas and clearly communicate priorities. A leader can have all the other attributes and skills required, but without the ability to clearly communicate, they will fail. If you have a strong candidate who is deficient in communication skills, get them into a training program to improve this ability.

Build and Protect the Brand

Three Roles Leaders Play in Your Firm

You work hard to build your firm and serve your clients. Once you grow beyond being a single proprietor, you will need to find, groom, and inspire a leadership team. Every leader in the organization has three key roles to play. They need to be Guardians, Champions, and Protectors of your firm and brand.

Three key roles every leader should play:

Guardian
Champion
Protector

GUARDIANS: Every firm has a brand. Firms with a brand rooted in deep values do best over the long run. They are self-confident about who they are, their clients pay to access the results produced by them, and their successful culture attracts top talent.

It takes effort, energy, and investment to organically grow a powerful brand. You have to pay attention to it. It is your leadership team's responsibility to be the guardians of your brand. The only sustainable advertising or promotion comes from out-innovating the competition. With better-quality solutions, better service, keen attentiveness, and more knowledge of the customer's industry, you win.

Leaders must understand the brand, share it, and strengthen it. The best leadership teams respect the value of a high-performing brand and know that laziness in caring for it will slowly destroy it. They are serious about being a brand's guardian.

CHAMPIONS: Every time you successfully deliver for a client and your firm, you are building value into your firm. Once you have done this for a while, you build up a reputation. You begin to have a legacy of value creation that fuels the worth of your brand, opens up new markets, and becomes your calling card. Leaders take on the role of being champions of your firm's legacy. They go out, spread the word, and let potential clients and talent know that your firm is passionate about delivering great work. Build on your next generation of leaders' skills in advocacy, communication, and being exceptional brand champions.

PROTECTORS: Building up an excellent reputation is hard work. As your firm grows, the number of people who represent your brand increases. When you have great guardians and champions, you will be well positioned to grow and continue the success story.

Every firm faces difficult challenges, such as people who get greedy, take shortcuts, and damage your firm's reputation. How can you protect against these types destroying all your hard work? The leaders you develop must demonstrate the highest levels of integrity and be passionate about defending the reputation of the firm. They are the protectors of your firm's reputation.

Take a Look:

Consistency

In the early days of our growth, we had lessons to learn about branding. As we increased the number of projects, people, and offices, we were doing pitches every day.

Our challenge: each professional was crafting a new and unique pitch. Each presentation looked completely different from every other. Because we had no consistency, we were not building our brand.

Once we realized this, we worked hard to build a consistent approach. Today we have a clear and strong brand.

Emotional Strength

Leadership is more than just certain core skills and essential attributes. It also calls on individuals to demonstrate both strength and grit.

Strength

Competition is a powerful driver. It compels us to do our best or risk being driven out of business. It pushes us to be inventive, create new services, and to be committed to delivering consistent value to our clients. We admire top-performing athletes, musicians, and professionals. What ties them all together is strength. I am not talking about brute power, but about strength of character. For me, strength is the will to be consistently better, to adhere to high ethical standards, and to support your team.

Unfortunately, some professionals give competition a bad reputation. It is all about ego. They fail to give their best, they take illegal shortcuts, and they are selfish. These people think they are strong, but actually, they are weak. As you build your leadership teams, make sure that they exhibit true strength.

"Look at your employees' toughest problems and make yourself part of the solution."

— UNKNOWN

Grit

Times can get tough—sometimes downright brutal. Our firm has been in business for 50 years through both boom and bust cycles. I have witnessed the fall of some organizations and the rise of others. From time to time, unanticipated environmental and political changes dramatically altered the way we did business. Through it all, our management team had the responsibility to lead the firm. We had to serve our clients and to protect both our work family and our own families. Every generation experiences these ups and downs.

Down times and periods of uncertainty ultimately demonstrate what kind of culture you have built in your firm. The companies I have seen struggle, fight, and emerge on the other side of difficult times are the ones where the leadership and internal culture exhibited grit.

Grit is an essential ingredient in your leadership team. When you are recruiting and considering a person for a leadership position, ask them to describe challenges they have faced. See how they handled outright failure. Did they drive ahead? Did they make tough decisions that were painful in the short run, but necessary for the survival of their team? Did they do this over and over again? If yes, they have grit. I respect grit in others. You should too.

Be Tough but Fair

A Decision-Maker's Life

As an owner or leader of a business or group, you are faced with making decisions all day long. It is how you make and deliver them that will define how successful you are. Businesses face pressures from every direction, meaning you will have to make difficult decisions. The key is to be consistently tough, fair, and reasonable.

In Dealing with Your Team

Service companies are in the business of people. We are well aware that people are complex and emotional. As a manager, it can be difficult to deliver negative news—such as telling an employee they will not get a raise; or addressing someone's need to build new skills before getting a promotion; or, of course, laying off an employee. There are other tough tasks to tackle as well, including mediating between internal groups facing a challenge, or asking senior managers to forgo bonuses during lean times. It is impossible to make everyone happy all the time. If you try, you will fail due to internal politics, and ultimately your team will fail to respect you. While it might be uncomfortable to be tough and to explain why your decision is in the best interests of everyone involved, being honest will build your team's respect and trust for you.

Clients

Being tough but fair also applies to clients. Service professionals often face clients who make unreasonable requests or behave inappropriately. If a client reaches beyond the scope of the agreed-upon deal so that you are running the project at a loss, you need to stand firm and work toward finding a solution that works for both parties. If you let the fear of losing the client drive you to make poor decisions, you will set a bad precedent.

"Talent never wears out.
Make weakness
irrelevant."

— PETER DRUCKER

Once you let a client take advantage of you, you will find it difficult to recover a healthy relationship or to retain the respect of your team. On occasion, a client might even verbally abuse someone on your team. As a leader, you must make it clear to your client that you expect mutual respect. If they threaten or bully you or your people, then it is better to move on and seek other clients.

Return on Respect

By being tough but fair, you set a clear standard. People will understand how you operate, know what you expect of others, and respect you for being fair. Long-term relationships with clients and low turnover in your team are two of the best possible returns on respect. Combined, they are the bedrock of building a long-term business venture.

Be Resilient

Knocked Down, Not Out

Because business is continually throwing you challenges, you may not always make the right decision. You will not always win the deal. Favorable markets can turn stormy, and you can get battered or sometimes outright knocked down. But don't succumb to a full knockout. Those who get back into the game are the ones who have learned the power of resilience. They are the ones who ultimately survive and thrive.

Do Not Be Afraid to Fail

If you want to live a full life and build a business or career, it is inevitable that you will experience some failures along the way. Do not be afraid of it. Fear makes you a slave; it stops you from experimenting and expanding. You will stagnate and eventually be out of business.

Stay Calm and Be Mindful

The best possible way to tame fear is to understand the risks involved in your endeavor and figure out how to

"Getting it wrong is part of getting it right."

— UNKNOWN

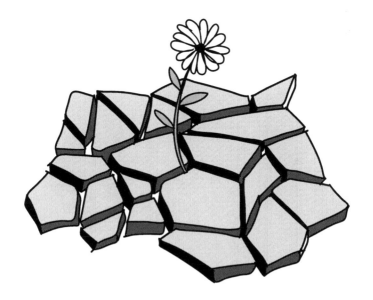

"A leader is interested in finding the best way—not in having his own way."

— JOHN WOODEN

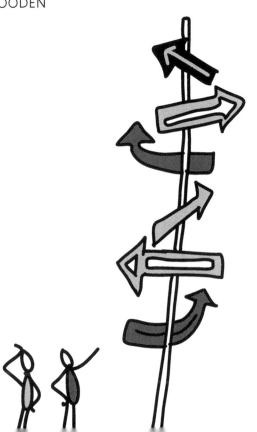

minimize them. Then, when something unanticipated appears, you can remain calm. Panic clouds your mind and makes it difficult to apply your problem-solving skills to work out a solution.

Many systems exist for building your skills at being mindful and calm, from focusing on the positive rather than the negative, to taking a few deep breaths and counting to 25, to the more evolved practices of yoga or meditation. Find one that works for you and practice it day in and day out. Eventually it will become your default emotional response to difficult times. It is always the calm and clear-headed ones who survive times of crisis.

Look Forward
When failure occurs, sift through it for any lessons to be learned. Too many people dwell on the past and burn up precious energy that could otherwise be invested in moving on and finding new opportunities. Put your energy into looking forward.

Accept. Adapt. Advance.
The ultimate keys to resiliency are to accept, to adapt, and to advance:

• Accept that you lost an opportunity or made a mistake. Spend no time making excuses or lingering around a lost opportunity. By accepting it, you can try to understand it. When you lose an opportunity, consider who won and what you could do differently next time. If you lose an employee, ask what you could do better next time to retain other employees. When the market changes, speak with others to see what new possibilities might be emerging.

- Adapt to your new circumstances. Take a hard look at your situation. Evaluate your skills, resources, and position. Focus on finding a new niche or possible solution. Your adaptations for survival might be substantial. This could mean trimming staff or cutting budgets. It might mean accepting smaller or less interesting projects. Ultimately, those who remain calm and figure out how to create value, even in stormy times, will be the ones who are strongest when good times return.

- Advance in tough times. Take advantage of what could be a favorable moment to move ahead. While others are panicking, you can pick up clients, new territories, and great talent. Your clients often go through the same rough periods as you. Stay focused on serving them in any way you can. They will remember that you supported them in the bad times and will be with you when the good times return. Build into your firm a culture of resilience.

Succession Planning

The Test of Time

Most professional services firms, especially small ones, come and go with the founder. Some make it into a second generation, and only a few go on to thrive into the third generation and beyond. One of the main culprits is the failure of the leadership team to embrace succession planning.

The roadblocks to succession include the following:

- Ego is the main roadblock. Most founders and leaders worked hard for their success. The thought of having to give it up or seeing their time at the helm

Life will still exist outside of work.

end triggers a deep emotional reaction. Leaders tell themselves that they alone know what is best for their company. It takes maturity to set aside one's ego and think about what is best for the long-term health of the organization.

- Fear of the unknown is another roadblock. Founders and leaders spend so much time doing their best to shape the future and manage the risks for the company that they have a hard time imagining what they will do when they retire. Over the years, I have heard founders and leaders tell me, "It's over." I ask them what they mean, and they answer, "Life." That is absolutely not true. So much life exists outside of work. The key is for the founders/leaders to find other meaningful activities outside their business life—such as time with family, community involvement, engaging hobbies, and so on. These offer a bright, rewarding retirement.

- Failure to embrace succession planning as early as possible creates another roadblock. Leaders often delay making plans until the last moment, and this will destroy a company every time.

Plan Sooner Rather Than Later

It always amazes me that, when it comes to succession planning, most technical experts take a wait-and-react approach. Professional services firms are in the business of providing advice. This advice helps design a bright future and attempts to steer clear of the pitfalls for their clients. Procrastination is an organization killer. By starting the succession-planning process early, you give yourself and your company the greatest chance to implement a successful transition from generation to generation.

The Talent Transition
The first element to a successful transition is to find the right people for the job. I encourage you to look internally for candidates. However, if you look externally, do it early so that you can recruit candidates into your firm and help them understand your firm's culture.

Once you have identified the pool of candidates, observe how they operate in a variety of situations. Give them tough assignments. Watch how they lead and treat people in good times and bad. Early planning is important because observation of your candidates takes time. When the transition is about to occur, you will have a tried and tested pool of leadership candidates who can rise to the challenge.

Client Conversion
In the professional services market, many relationships with your company start with a specific person. Many times, employees are as loyal to one person, a trusted

advisor, as they are to the brand. This is especially true at the founder and leadership level.

It is important at every level to build a strong tie to the firm's brand and to create a community of trusted advisors for your clients. When the transition time comes, your clients will already have built up some trust with the other advisors. As you transition, you can step back and give the upcoming advisor a greater opportunity to deepen ties with clients. This serves the client well, helps the firm continue to grow, and keeps the leader's reputation intact as someone who cares about their client's future success.

No Financial Plan to Support Leaving

Many founders/leaders assume they will work forever and thus do not plan for retirement. They do not save for the occasion, nor does the firm put money aside to buy out their ownership. Both issues need to be addressed. I recommend that a profit sharing or 401(k) program be established and money be allowed to accumulate until they retire.

As for the buyout, I recommend an ESOP (Employee Stock Ownership Plan). Selling the firm to another company destroys all you have built. If you care about your people and want to assure their long-term future, selling out is not the best way to go. Leaving the firm with a

ART'S PRINCIPLES

debt and repayment schedule to retire your ownership is not much better. Plan ahead and you will have a successful leadership and ownership transition.

Quietly Transition

Many firms make a huge media splash when they transition leadership teams. I actually encourage a quiet transition. Doing a major public announcement puts unnecessary pressure on the new team. All external and internal eyes are now watching to see what happens next.

The transition itself can take time. Going from managing a slice of the organization to running a greater piece comes with growing pains. A quiet transition gives space for the new leadership to settle into their jobs.

A quiet transition is also good for your clients. Change makes everyone nervous. The clients will wonder whether they will receive the same quality advice and the same level of service. By quietly making the transition, you take a more personalized approach toward making your clients aware of the changes, and give them a preview of some of the positive changes to come. Ultimately, you give the new leadership a chance to become the trusted advisor that your clients and employees have come to expect at your company.

Take a Look:

Start Early

In my case, I started to plan for succession of leadership early in the formation of the firm. I always felt that I couldn't ask someone to commit their professional career to an organization that had no long-term plans for its future leadership. It seemed unfair. I also was concerned about how I could receive a fair return for my ownership of the firm. I did not believe in putting the firm in debt to buy me out or to pay me over the following years. I especially believed that long-term payouts to me in my absence put leadership in the position of worrying about how to make the necessary payments rather than focusing on the business.

I did not want to be subject to the vagaries of the economy. The firm's leaders decided to fund an ESOP that could purchase the stock at fair market value when I stepped down. It was also important that the transition from one leadership group to the next be seamless. In our case, I was the original owner. Later, we moved to a combination of my ownership plus three others with smaller but significant ownership.

Along the way, we have gifted all of our principals with stock ownership. As they developed into full leaders, one became vice-chairman and another became president. I had been president, CEO, and chairman. Gradually, I passed on the role of president, then CEO, and was only the chairman.

Over a period of a few years, those three retired, and the next group of six were selected as an executive committee to start the following succession process. After a period of five or six years, they gradually took over total control of the firm, with three becoming the executive directors and all six on the executive committee. During this entire period, we also had a management committee with rotating members to provide input on operational issues.

Now I am a part-time employee with no leadership responsibilities. The firm purchased my stock ownership through the ESOP.

I have also been an active member on the boards of a series of not-for-profit organizations. Serving on the executive committee of three energetic boards now keeps me busy and gratified.

I am confident this long-term approach has allowed the firm to build a transition process that ensures the organization's continuation long into the future. The leadership team is compensated fairly for their efforts. The slow transition process has provided ample time for the team to experience some good and bad economic times and to develop the skills to handle both.

Talent

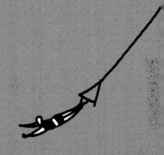

Hire the Best

The Power of Hiring

Hiring the right people is one of the most important skills you need as a business owner or leader. When you get the right person for the right position at the right time, it creates an ability to thrive. Professionals look for careers, not jobs. Create an environment where your people can grow and build their skills.

Talent is critical. Become a student of hiring. Develop a recruitment strategy. Be a magnet for talent. The problem is that people often hire the wrong person at the wrong time for the wrong reasons. When you do this, you encourage disaster.

Being the Best

Hire the best talent you can afford. Ask yourself: How do you define being the best? Is it about finding the most competent technical expert? Is it about finding people with years of relevant experience? Yes and no. Yes, you want to find skilled talent. Yes, a strong track record is ideal. Does this equate to being the best? Not necessarily.

"Hire the best athletes. A willingness to take chances. An ability to generate original ideas. An active curiosity."

— TOM LANDRY

Technical expertise is not the only answer. Make sure you offer projects and opportunities that will instill in your new employees a drive for excellence and opportunity. You must also offer reasonable compensation and benefits to reap the success of an organization where everybody is pulling together to build a world-class firm.

Beyond the Basics
While most people make the mistake of singling out technical skills as the most important attribute, I think a person must have two other attributes in order to be considered the best: good character and the ability to be a team player.

When hiring, consider not only whether the candidates can do the job, but also whether they will continue to grow as the organization grows. If your people are preoccupied with only themselves, they may be more prone to unethical behavior. If they focus on who they are now, plus who they want to be in the future, they will behave ethically.

Content of Your Character
Character is the bedrock of people. It drives their decision-making and how they treat others. A person's character can strengthen your firm's culture or poison it. Discovering the content of a person's character during the interview process is extremely important.

When you evaluate a person's character, look for five qualities before hiring them:

- Look for drive. You want people who are passionate about their profession. They should be excited to wake up, jump into action, and make an impact on a daily basis. Eliminate people who just punch the clock, dread their jobs, and are in it only for the paycheck.

- Look for confidence, as it enables a person to take an expansive view on life. Confidence fuels curiosity and leads to new possibilities. People who lack confidence usually have a narrow perspective. They let fear envelop them, keeping them from exploring or dealing with change.

- Discipline must be coupled with passion and confidence. You are running a business. Make sure your people have the focus and commitment it takes to deliver on promises to clients.

- New hires must know right from wrong. It is non-negotiable. Jack Welch's motto was, "Do not do anything you wouldn't want to show up on the front page of the newspaper." Trust is hard to earn and easily destroyed by bad behavior. Keep your firm strong by bringing in people who do the right thing.

- Finally, it is so important to seek people who demonstrate that making a difference in the world matters to them, both at work and outside of it. Inquire about which charitable and philanthropic issues are important to them. Do they volunteer? Are there issues that they are passionate about and are proactively trying to improve?

Teamwork

Most professional services firms are small because they do not know how to build effective teams. Look for talent with experience playing team sports, being part of musical groups, or being involved in charitable projects. Ask potential hires to describe their team experiences. Observe whether they acknowledge the contributions of others, or are egocentric. Seek people who love being part of a team versus feeling trapped by it.

Even if you take the smallest unit of a single service provider and a single client, you see a team dynamic. As you build a firm at scale, the one way to avoid the plague of a "Me vs. Us" attitude is to be certain that you have talent whose default approach is teamwork.

Attract and Keep Talent

Hire People Smarter Than You

Do you want to go beyond being a solo entrepreneur? Do you want your firm to become great? As a group leader, do you want to expand or improve? In all these instances, you will need to attract and keep talented people.

While you seek to recruit the right talent for the right position at the right time, one question you should always ask yourself is: Is this person smarter than I am? They might not be smarter than you in your area of

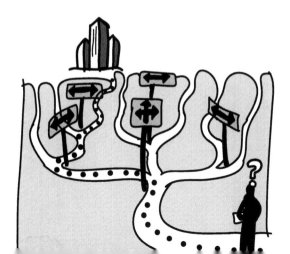

expertise, but stronger in another area. Does hiring this individual raise the bar for your organization? Will they bring that special expertise to your organization?

Put aside your ego and ask probing questions to determine whether they are smarter than you are. By surrounding yourself with smart people, you have the best chance of consistently creating value for your clients. A bright and intelligent new employee can supply the talent your organization needs in areas where you are not an expert.

Responsibility plus Authority

Very smart people want to make use of their talents. They are hungry for responsibility and welcome the chance to flex their minds. Challenging assignments give them an opportunity to grow.

You should do everything possible to empower talent to serve your clients and represent your firm in the most positive way possible. The key to unlocking your talents' potential is to make sure they are given the authority they need to succeed. Authority enables them to access resources and make decisions that help advance the firm.

Some managers are afraid to empower others. If you are one of these leaders, I suggest you offer levels of authority. As your talent makes wise decisions, you can grant greater levels of authority. Always match the responsibilities you give them with the right amount of authority to get the job done.

Keep Your Word
Finding the right talent is one thing, retaining it is another. The single best way to keep your talent is to keep your word. Talented employees want to understand what it takes for them to perform, grow within the firm, and succeed. It is your responsibility to make sure they understand what is required.

Be candid about it. Living by your words creates authenticity. This is the only way a true merit system takes root and thrives. Meritocracy is absolutely the best way to consistently attract outstanding talent year after year. It has worked for our firm for the past 50 years.

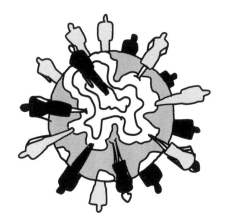

(22)

Invest in Your People

When a good athlete successfully jumps over the high bar, what does a good coach do? First, celebrate the accomplishment, then raise the bar. Focus on strengths. Coaches show only winning plays, not where failure has occurred. Visualize winning.

Your Team Is Your Business
Your talent is your business in the professional services world. As an owner or leader, you are responsible for making sure that your firm is investing in its talent.

Start Training Right Away
If you are just starting out, you might think that investing

in your people is a luxury. You are mistaken. It is a necessity. Make it a priority as a sole proprietor and on through the time you become a large-scale organization.

Even when I was starting out and cash was tight, I found ways to bring in experts to help us improve. I worked with a top lawyer, Dennis Rice. I had relationships with top engineering consultants, and early on I hired a professor, Glen Strasberg, to teach us business skills after-hours. Fortunately, today there are multitudes of online resources, many of them free. You have no excuse to avoid investing in your team from the beginning.

Get Everyone Involved
When you build your firm, make sure that a passion for self-improvement is part of the culture. By doing this, you lay the groundwork to activate everyone as an educator. Senior talent can take on the mentor role, but as you bring young talent onboard, they can serve as reverse mentors by exposing senior members to new technologies and new trends.

Learn from Athletic Teams
When we think about investing in our people, we often approach it much like sports coaches would with their teams. The coaches with the best track records often have surprisingly straightforward workout regimens

for their players. They understand that for every sport, there is a core program that serves as the fundamental building blocks for achieving high performance at game time. They know it takes a constant and consistent investment in everyone on the team getting these fundamentals right in order to produce season after season of victories.

Core Professional Services Regimen
There are three ways to invest in the education of your talent. This applies to all professional services firms.

INVEST IN CROSS-TRAINING: While you want your talent to be deep in one area of expertise, it is equally important that they have a solid understanding of how other groups work within your firm. By encouraging different groups to collaborate through learning activities, you create major benefits. Both your talent and your firm become resilient. Markets come and go, and the pace at which this happens is getting faster and faster. Cross-training helps you navigate this reality. The better cross-trained your people are, the more likely they will be able to adapt and adjust to new opportunities once the old ones no longer exist.

Also, collaboration efforts improve your team. Cross-training creates meaningful experiences between different groups within your firm. It avoids silo thinking and builds up a pool of trust among your people. The results of collaboration are always good. People who trust each other and have a better understanding of one another's capabilities are much more likely to spot potential business opportunities, and are more motivated to generate a referral.

OFFER FIELD EXPERIENCE: Nothing beats real-life learning. Over time, I discovered the power of having fresh talent or recently appointed managers join our client pitches and meetings. While they were silent observers at external meetings, it gave them a front-row seat on the action. It also showed our potential and current clients that we invest in our people.

In a meeting, I would explain that this person was joining us, at our expense, and then showcase that person's great energy and potential. This helped build both confidence and excitement among clients, because it showed we cared, and it gave them a preview of the talent we recruited at our firm. It also inspired self-confidence in the individual.

REQUIRE MEANINGFUL CONTINUING EDUCATION CREDITS (required for all professional services fields): Because the programs can be boring and seem like squandered time, I suggest you transform them. Have your firm team up with an accredited agency that can issue continuing education credits. Make the courses exciting and relevant to your talent's day-to-day work life by tapping into your senior talent to help design the programs. If you are just starting out and have limited resources, make sure to invest your energies in curating high-quality continuing education opportunities.

Keep Them Coming Back for More

It is true that finding, recruiting, and retaining talent is exceptionally hard work. The most frightening reality about building a professional services firm is that your most valuable assets walk out the door every night. If you want to retain your talent and have them excited to return in the morning, you need to invest in them. It will be one of the best decisions you ever make as a business owner or a team leader.

Take a Look:

Continue
the Education

About our third year in business, I realized I knew
very little about the business side of the architectural
profession. I decided to take an evening continuing education course at the University of California
Extension Program.

A few weeks into the class, I acknowledged that not
only did I need to learn the principles being discussed, but that my team also should hear and learn
them. Consequently, I hired the professor to come to
our office after work to teach all of us. When he gave
us homework, we all met weekly to review and get
further instruction. Our team learned the principles
of leading and running a professional services firm,
and the professor ultimately became a key consultant
to our industry.

Earn the Title

A Lean and Flat Organization

I encourage you to build a lean and flat organization rooted in meritocracy. Because a flat organization means fewer steps to the top, it liberates your firm from the clutter of meaningless titles.

Flat organizations keep the focus on the firm's excellence and what it does, not on how to get higher up in the organization. The client needs to be served by the proper person regardless of what that person's title is. Ultimately, each title is significant. People in lean organizations know they have to earn their title through consistent results.

House Rules

Anyone you bring into the organization must adhere to the house rules that guide your culture. They need to understand what it takes to help the family and to demonstrate their worth. Titles have meaning only if you respect the person.

No Titles for Lateral Hires

I advocate having no titles for lateral hires for the first year. This applies to entry-level positions up to senior management. Though this practice is often difficult for people to accept, we have resisted their complaints. In some cases, they were senior partners in their former organizations and didn't want to accept what they perceived to be a demotion.

Our position was that it would take at least a year for them to truly understand our family culture and our ways of working and serving clients. If they were not

ready to accept the policy, then perhaps they were not the right hire for the firm. But the people who did accept our position ultimately appreciated our approach and embraced it.

This approach helps the new hire go native to your culture. They earn the respect of their colleagues based on merit and teamwork done cooperatively versus forced authority brought in from experience at their former employment. Those hires willing to embrace this method also indicate a commitment to be champions of the brand, not just their own careers.

Once the year is over, the appropriate fit or title can be applied. It will feel organic and rooted in a team consensus. This goes far in keeping a strong culture oriented toward long-term growth.

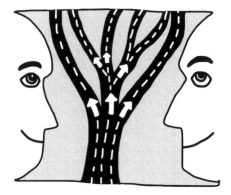

Guide Your Talent

This and That

Since service companies are in the talent-management business, it means the company must figure out how to balance three major tensions.

LONG-TERM AND SHORT-TERM VIEW: The first challenge to navigate is the balancing act between the long-term and the short-term mindset. Your talent must integrate both into their daily decision-making. The long term means being at the leading edge of your industry. This is how you retain your clients and win new ones. It means innovating, expanding into new geographies, and acquiring new skills.

Long-term thinking makes business effective, but it is not always efficient. The short-term view keeps your talent committed to being exceptionally productive. It means meeting deadlines, and performing on budget and on scope.

I think the best way to achieve this is by "open book" management. Help your team understand the firm's strategic vision as well as its financial fitness through frequent updates. We value what we measure, so we try to provide detailed reports to our managers and leaders. We measure the productivity of our professional staff, collections, performance-to-project budget, and many other areas.

WE vs. ME: The second biggest challenge is balancing the individual's ambitions with those of the firm. You must determine whether you want an army of mercenaries or want to build a firm that acts as a family.

We personally believe in building a family culture. Families have staying power and build deep roots. A family culture respects both the individual and the group, and is committed to helping each other out. You celebrate in the good times, and you cooperate to figure out your way forward during the tough ones. Whichever model you choose, your mission is to align the ambitions so that both can thrive.

ENGAGE AND REFRESH: Whether you are a big firm or a small one, make sure your talent takes the time needed to refresh themselves. Today there is much discussion about avoiding burnout. I am not a fan of the term "burnout" because it somehow gives work a negative connotation. Good work brings purpose and meaning to people's lives. I am more in favor of people "refreshing" themselves.

This shifts the conversation from "How do I lighten my daily workload?" to "How do I make the most of my rejuvenation time?" Rejuvenation is more than relaxing and forgetting about work. It is ensuring that you are healthy, are learning new things, and are meeting new people.

True rejuvenation provides an opportunity to rethink your job. It lets you see your career from a different perspective. A fresh look might help you devise new ways to assist your client or make suggestions that could improve their business.

Successful firms encourage their people to rejuvenate themselves. It is the only way the talent can consistently do well over the long run. I believe in taking the long view on your talent's well-being.

"A person might make mistakes, but he or she isn't a failure until he or she starts blaming someone else."

— JOHN WOODEN

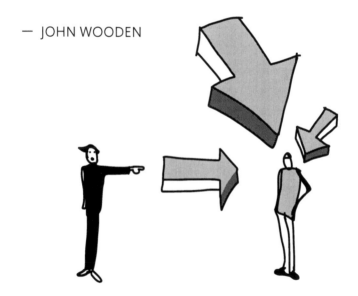

Take a Look:

Rejuvenate and Refresh

I have used the process of rejuvenation in several ways. I find, especially as I get older, that I need to take breaks. My wife and I have traveled the world, many times with the San Francisco Chamber of Commerce Trade and Good Will missions to major cities in Europe, Russia, Africa, and Asia. We have also visited Washington, D.C., with the Chamber to meet with our government representatives and the President in the White House.

In traveling with some of the most interesting and influential people, we have found these trips to be wonderful personal and educational experiences. We have also toured with the San Francisco Museum of Modern Art to many cities in Europe and Asia, meeting people in each of the countries and learning about their interests and activities.

Our travels were unlike a typical lying-on-the-beach vacation and were certainly more vigorous, but the experiences have enriched my life and my self-confidence.

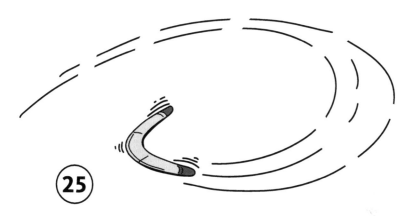

(25)
Boomerang

Stay in the Family

Professional services firms are always on a mission to find high-quality talent. It requires time, effort, and financial resources to locate, train, and bring someone onboard. It takes even more time, shared experiences, and commitment for the talent to transform into a member of your firm's family.

Being a family member means that they understand your approach toward business and the principles that drive your culture. Eventually, with experience, they become true members of the family. They put the firm first, help other members of the family, and do their best to consistently create value for clients.

When this happens with a new employee, it is gratifying. You want them to stay and be part of the family for as long as possible. You want them to build a career with you. Unfortunately, it does not always turn out that way.

Change Happens
Perhaps a spouse gets an opportunity in another city where your firm doesn't have an office. Maybe your team member receives an offer with new possibilities that they cannot refuse. It could be that someone wants to go back to school, explore a social venture, or travel. The fact is that change occurs, and your talent will leave your firm.

Boomerangs
What happens when that opportunity in another city fails to pan out? What if that new firm falls short of your former talent's commitment to excellence? What if the sabbatical wraps up early? Life can also change in this way.

For most professional services firms, when people leave, they do not return. It might be that the talent feels there is no longer a place for them at their former firm. Or they might feel awkward that things did not work out at their new job. Or they might worry that they traveled for too long. The talent may have personal reasons for not returning, but the fact is that it could very well be a company issue.

Talent may leave...

...but talent may also return.

Welcome Them Back

If you employ highly talented, value-creating people who want to try something new, it is your responsibility to let them know that you would welcome them back to the family. However, be selective about the talent you welcome back into the firm. We call the folks we welcome back "boomerangs." About five percent of our firm consists of boomerangs. The positive is that they already understand your culture, know what level of excellence your clients expect, understand your operations, and return quickly to producing value.

Take a Look:

A Fun Gift

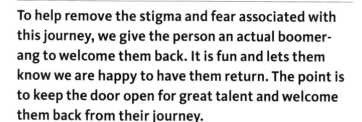

To help remove the stigma and fear associated with this journey, we give the person an actual boomerang to welcome them back. It is fun and lets them know we are happy to have them return. The point is to keep the door open for great talent and welcome them back from their journey.

When to Let Go

Learn to Let Go

Learning to let talent go is one of the toughest challenges for a leader. Good leaders love to hire talent, to see them perform well, and to reward them for their good results. No one enjoys firing people or letting people go.

In our companies, we have all faced the giant egos, blamers, or people who find drama in every situation. Even if these types are tremendously talented, they have an incredibly negative impact on your people. If you let them continue with this behavior, you cannot expect the rest of the team to respect you or your firm.

Today we live in a world where the pace of change is so fast that the skills needed to succeed are soon eclipsed by what is needed to serve tomorrow's clients. To remain viable, your firm must be aware of coming changes and prepare the organization for them as soon as possible. Changes may necessitate letting certain talent go, for the good of both that employee and your firm.

Leaps in the Market
Because markets are dynamic, even the most boring industries experience change. There comes a time when a market leaps forward. This could be due to external market demands or even factors within your internal marketplace. Sometimes you are faced with a major economic decline or a recession, locally or nationally.

Although all companies would like to have a no-lay-off policy, it is unfair to the health of the firm and to the employees who remain to support those with no work. Do your best to assign other projects, but if that doesn't succeed, then you must face the challenge of leading your firm through the difficult times.

Your job as a leader is to understand the circumstances and to take action that positions your firm to succeed as it goes forward. Take a thorough look at your talent and determine who will be ready for the leap and who will need to be laid off.

Shifting Skill Sets

With these market changes, there will be shifts in the skills required to thrive. Some of your talent will adjust, adapt, and be able to serve your emerging clients. Others will resist or reject the new reality and fail to upgrade their skills. You must let them go. The difficult people to lay off are the talent who truly wish to participate in the new market. Though they show enthusiasm, commitment, and an effort to adapt, for whatever reason, they are unable to shift their skills to meet the new reality.

The truth is that your talent wants something they cannot find in your firm or industry. They can be disgruntled or unhappy. As a leader, you need to let them go before they poison your firm's culture, and so they can move into a field or firm where they find satisfaction and success. It is your responsibility to help them by letting them go while they still have a chance for success. If you do not relieve them, your younger talent will move on to where they can continue to grow.

Time to Do Something Else

Sometimes a talented employee plateaus or becomes stuck in a rut. If you respect this person and they are helpful to your clients, do your best to find them new assignments, let them participate in opening up new marketplaces, or give them opportunities to build new skills. The issue is that sometimes people simply have peaked within your organization. Eventually, they become chronically vocal to their colleagues about their dissatisfaction. Because negativity is contagious, these people are dangerous to your organization's morale.

Need for New Challenges

We have had situations where outstanding people were failing in their current assignments. We moved them to another geographic location, where they blossomed. Try to determine their difficulties and provide them with a totally new experience. In these cases, many have remained with our firm for years, and have again made excellent contributions.

Help Your Talent Plan for the Future

Discover What's Next

The "boomer" tsunami is heading toward its crest. Leaders are being forced to look at a dramatically changing landscape in their workforces. Waves of talent will be retiring. Your talent is asking: "What does it mean to retire?"

Because most folks are living longer now, an entire third chapter of life opens up for people to explore both professionally and personally. If you want to be a great firm, you will help your talent envision what it means to retire. You will help them discover the potential to have a brilliant third chapter.

Step Forward

Our society has yet to catch up to the fact that we live so long. While more years can be a positive, it is important that those years are meaningful and full of engagement. The idea that retirees will sit around or play golf all day is an outdated concept.

You want your talent stepping forward into a world of new possibilities. This can include nonprofit activities, mentoring a young venture, starting up a small business, or taking up a hobby.

Start Sooner Rather Than Later
Usually people defer thinking about retirement until just before they actually retire. That sets the stage for disorientation, boredom, and sometimes depression. If you have high-performing, talented individuals, you want them to be engaged in life. And yes, they might take that long-awaited trip around the world and indulge in a few rounds of golf. However, most people wake up shortly after their official retirement and ask what is next.

Encourage internal company conversation around the topic, and do it sooner rather than later. Also, do the same for yourself. When it is time for you to step aside, make sure you have the talent in place to lead the next generation. Ensuring a positive succession is one of your most important jobs.

"What a group does with its billable time determines its income for the year.

"What it does with its nonbillable time determines its future."

— DAVID MAISTER
Managing the Professional Service Firm

Start having conversations a year before your older talent is set to retire. Conducting workshops and learning opportunities to explore life after the firm will help your talent embrace their next chapter. Your people will be excited about what comes in retirement. That translates into positive energy within the firm, which then promotes good morale.

Stay Connected
Encourage your retired talent to stay linked with the firm and with each other. You can do this formally via a newsletter or alumni events. Retirees can informally maintain relationships with their former fellow employees. My advice is simply to stay connected with them.

Alumni can be outstanding brand ambassadors. They can help you recruit fresh talent, they can mentor people, and they can help channel your current talent into volunteering opportunities with the charities where they may be involved. Alumni can also maintain connections with their past clients. This creates a virtuous cycle of attracting, grooming, and keeping great talent.

Daily Work Life

(28) Curiosity

Always Be Curious

While many firms emphasize recruiting for intelligence, I think they should equally consider factoring in curiosity. Intelligence sums up how effective you are at problem-solving, and signals how much expert knowledge you have stockpiled. This combination helps people evaluate your technical capabilities as a service professional.

On the other hand, curiosity signals how hungry you are to learn new things and how wide your range of interests is. The stronger your curiosity, the more fields you will explore. The more you explore, the more you are likely to find innovative solutions and excel at cross-pollination.

No Filter

Our days are filled with finding answers to specific problems with a defined set of filters. At the end of the day's work, I suggest feeding your curiosity. I also encourage you to remove your standard filters. Filters can be everything from the way we always do something, to long-term biases that are, in fact, old-way thinking.

If you are in the legal field, read something that has to do with architecture. If you are a designer, investigate education. Attend lectures that expand your vision of the world. Engage in conversations with people outside of your industry. In doing so, you will become a more interesting person and a better professional, because you can apply new insights to your field that are learned from others.

50/50

I have a routine of reading in the evenings. About half of my reading is drawn from my industry, and the other half covers many fields of interest. I also engage with 100 percent of my clients in educational conversations.

In the past five decades, I have had a front-row seat at the rise and fall of industries. Some clients retool themselves while entire new fields pop up. If you are genuinely curious and become a good listener, you will always be at the leading edge of your industry as a service professional.

Unanticipated Discoveries
While some people read to retrieve specific information, I often do not know what I am looking for. By skipping the filters and feeding my curiosity, I stumble upon unanticipated discoveries. It might be an advertisement or a chapter in a book. It could be a TED Talk, a technical article, or even just a piece of art.

Year after year, these discoveries produce a more complete map of the world. The better your map is, the better able you are to position your firm as a problem solver to potential and current clients.

Share It
Spread your curiosity by selecting meaningful items to share. If you proactively share insights and articles, you will become a go-to source for employees, partners, and clients. This becomes contagious. Once others are affected by your actions, they will also begin to curate useful information and share it with you. This fuels everyone's ability to improve and become more success-ful in their respective fields.

"Leaders are people with a very poorly developed sense of fear and no real comprehension of the odds against them. They are people who make the impossible happen."

— ROBERT JARVIK
Inventor of the artificial heart

Ever-Smarter Sector

Remember, all boats rise in a rising tide. I think it is important to share your insights so that your sector becomes ever smarter. Some people argue that sharing will impact their competitiveness. As other firms adapt, your know-how will already be on the path to newer and better ways of doing things.

A great example is the recent move by Tesla. It wants everyone to manufacture better, smarter, and more environmentally friendly vehicles. As such, it announced it would open-source its patents. To be sure, Elon Musk is not sitting around waiting for his competition to outdo him. He is already working on his next innovation. The industry will only get better through sharing.

(29)
It's 6:00 p.m. Go Home!

Get a Life!

It is 6:00 p.m. Time to go! I mean it. The decisions you make about allocating your personal time will ultimately shape your life's strategy. All too often people equate working late into the night as a sign of commitment and as part of what it takes to get ahead. I think it is the opposite. Constantly working late into the night puts you on a dangerous path.

Burnout. Boring. Behind.

As I mentioned previously, I do not believe in burnout. If you do your job right, burnout won't exist. Your goal is to understand what it takes to get the job done, plan for it, and then be smart about doing it. Clocking in more hours is not the answer. If you consistently get this formula wrong, you will burn out. You need time to refuel.

The other danger is that you become boring. You need downtime to pursue activities that feed your passions. The pursuit of passions is what keeps you interested in life and interesting to others.

And, if you are always clocking in late hours and skipping vacations, you risk the chance of falling behind. It is by exploring the world around you that you spot new trends, spark new ideas, and have the mental space to noodle on new possibilities.

Mix It Up After 6:00 p.m.

Diversify your life and mix it up with people outside of your profession. If you work all day in one field and then hang out with the same people afterward, you run the risk of becoming insular, narrow, and stale. The same applies to how you feed your mind and home life. Be an explorer. Share what you discover with your friends, family, and colleagues. By doing this, you create the environment for discussing new ideas, pursuing new projects together, and spotting new trends.

Another positive aspect of exploring is that it makes you a healthier, more well-rounded person, and brings new ideas, energy, and possibilities to your daytime work. If you don't expand your life outside of work, your ability to contribute positively to your clients, your projects, your relationships, and your health quickly diminishes.

The 6:00 p.m. Stretch
Yes, there will be times when a client's project has an accelerated schedule or special requirements. You will need to be flexible and stretch past 6:00 p.m. The key is to avoid this becoming your standard operating procedure. Work on learning balance. Do not under-invest in your family and over-invest in your career. Family and friends are the most powerful and enduring source of happiness.

Take a Look:

Break When You Can

When the firm started, I only had one car. Every day I commuted the half-hour ride to my San Francisco office on the Tiburon ferry. On the morning ferry, I took the opportunity to get organized, have a cup of coffee, and read the paper. At the end of the workday, my clients and employees knew I needed to leave the office to catch the 5:30 p.m. ferry home.

Riding the ferry was a great way to get a break from work, see friends, and meet potential clients. Once home, my wife picked me up with our three boys and we enjoyed dinner together. When we finally got the boys to bed, I would often drive back to the city with my dog and do the layouts for the tenants I had met that day. The fact that I took the ferry break made it possible for me to keep that crazy schedule and survive.

(30)
Storytelling

You Are a Storyteller

Stories are powerful. They build understanding, commitment, and inspiration. Storytelling does not come naturally to everyone. If you plan to run your own business or assume a leadership position, you and your teammates need to become storytellers.

Develop Great Stories

Getting your message out into the world is one thing; doing it well is something else. I often see bright people overwhelm potential clients with industry babble. Using a multitude of technical words does not make you look smart. It makes you appear pretentious and leaves your clients dazed and confused.

Communicating from the audience's point of view is effective storytelling. Study your clients. Try to understand them and how they view the world. If you see their viewpoint, you have a much higher chance of entering a meaningful conversation to gain insight into their problem. Then you explain how you can create value by helping them fix it.

Share Your Stories
Ask your client what they do. First, you will learn about the person and their organization; and second, you will know what stories to share. Be sure to choose a story that fits the point you are trying to make.

You can be the world's best storyteller, but if you fail to spread your stories, no one will know you exist. Get out there and get some conversations started. The good news is that there are so many ways to communicate. For instance, you can develop a topic and speak at an industry conference, write an article for publication, or post your ideas on the Internet. Pick and choose the channels that work best for you and your audience.

It Is a Conversation
When you tell a story, understand that you are really involved in a conversation. Gone are the days when you spoke down to, up to, or at someone. I have always

thought it was so interesting to be engaged in a conversation, in contrast to simply broadcasting information. Everyone learns more. When you are in a powerful conversation, you discover new trends, find new commercial opportunities, and hear about talent that might be helpful to your firm.

One to a Million

With the arrival of social media, you can be storytelling—with one person or millions—with very few words. Social media has also dramatically changed how we tell stories. Everyone co-creates a story about you and your firm's brand. With that in mind, I suggest that you always keep your communications authentic, direct, and honest. Try to learn from every conversation. Accept that some people will love you and others will grumble. Through it all, keep at your storytelling.

Take a Look:

Steve Jobs

Steve Jobs was a masterful storyteller. This was not by accident, but by design. The first time I witnessed the power of his storytelling was on a panel we shared. I spoke about office design, and he talked about the future of computers. This was still in the early days of personal computers.

After the panel, Steve asked me to visit him at his one-story tilt-up office. When I arrived, I asked him again to explain to me why I would want a computer. He took out a floppy disk and displayed a spreadsheet program on the monitor. When he said that this was going to transform how people did business, I finally understood the value of a personal computer.

After showing me the program, we picked up some trail mix at a convenience store, went for a walk, and then settled on the lawn between the curb and the sidewalk. Here he painted for me a clear picture of the future of Apple. It was great storytelling.

He then asked us to design his offices to help him realize that vision. We worked together on most of his offices until he left Apple. Some years later, I received a call. "Hi, this is Steve Jobs." At first, I thought one of my buddies was playing a joke on me. Then I recognized the voice. It was Steve!

He had returned to Apple and needed direct distribution for his products. He wanted a retail store. I said, "Steve, you have only two products, desktop and laptop computers." He already had a clear vision. He wanted a place to tell the story of his future product lines—iPod, iPhone, and iPad—though he did not tell me then what they were.

He was intense and relentless, working and reworking his vision of the store. After doing his homework, he would become engrossed in the smallest of details to make sure they matched his vision. He was tough, but in the end, he was right. We went on to produce the first 100 stores with him. His stores told a story. The power of that storytelling produced the highest-grossing retail sales per square foot worldwide. Steve truly understood the importance of bringing masterful stories to all aspects of his business.

Build Your Own Career

Own Your Career

Have the guts to own your career. Refuse to play the victim. You have one life and what you do for a living makes up a large part of your time. Make the most of it. Make it joyful and rewarding. Develop a sense of purpose for what you are doing. What you do with your billable time will determine your income for the year. What you do with your nonbillable time will determine your future. It is your choice to build a successful career. Design your life and then lay the foundation for being able to generate consistent value over the years. Don't let your competition define you; make sure *you* define what *you* want to be.

Be Honest with Yourself

Successful careers are built on two simple building blocks. The first is creating value. The second is sharing it.

Most people find it difficult being totally honest with themselves about the value they create. If you think you can do it, you probably can. If you think you can't, you probably can't. Do not set yourself up for failure by saying you can't. You need to consistently adjust, adapt, and advance your abilities and know-how so that you are positioned to create value. Learn to execute, execute, execute.

Basic Building Blocks of Every Career

TECHNICAL SKILL AND KNOWLEDGE: The major requirement in building a successful career is to understand the field you are working in. Learn the language. Learn what makes it work. Question the status quo. Your education is a start, but with the rate of change in today's world, you will need to constantly upgrade it. Continued learning will give you the ability to systematically abandon yesterday in order to create tomorrow.

Your industry will always undergo changes. In fact, it might become totally disrupted and replaced by a wave of new ventures. The only way you will not get swept away is if you constantly learn and educate yourself about the world of possibilities and oncoming changes.

"The future will be what you decide to make it."

— TONY ROBBINS

Expanding your learning zone helps you avoid being trapped by conventional wisdom, which could be wrong and blind you. Exploring wider horizons positions you to be attuned to new prospects and helps you build new skills that can prove valuable.

EFFECTIVE COMMUNICATION: You can create value, but unless you can communicate it clearly, you may miss the opportunity to be rewarded for it. Invest your energies in being masterful at communicating across all media. This could be through tweeting, texting, emailing, speaking engagements, or the rare and always appreciated handwritten letter.

I would encourage everyone—even the shyest person— to focus the most attention on public speaking. Watch TED Talks, enroll in seminars, join Toastmasters, or learn from public speakers whom you admire and respect.

DISCIPLINE: The world is filled with smart people. All things being equal, discipline is the key long-term success factor. When you promise something, deliver it. If you hit roadblocks, find a reasonable alternative. It is essential to have the discipline to consistently deliver value.

ATTENTION TO THE CLIENT: If you do all of the above, but let your ego get in the way of serving the client, you will fail and your career will falter. The best careers are built on relinquishing your ego and focusing on the client's needs. While they pay the bills, you are there to serve them. In this case, your client is your boss and teammate. Create and communicate value, and you will have a long and fruitful career.

Success is an option. You must have the fortitude to choose it because you own your employability. Be more concerned with your character than your reputation: your character is what you really are, while your reputation is what other people think you are.

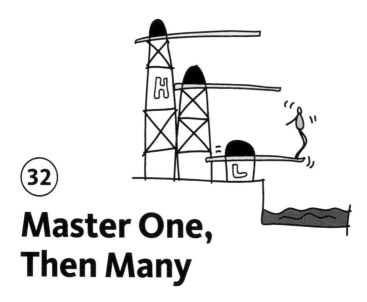

(32)

Master One,
Then Many

Mastery Matters

I am a strong advocate of having a broad range of
interests and skills that you acquire through curiosity
and the exploration of unknown territory. I am equally
a champion of mastery. To build a successful professional services firm, you must identify your niche, then
master it. Put in the time and effort it takes to become
exceptional at a niche that generates value for clients.
Mastery matters because that is what drives clients to
hire you and your organization.

Identify a niche and own it.

Many Skills

To move beyond being a one-skill leader or organization, you must build a team that embraces the mastery of many skills and a willingness to explore many others. I have found it advantageous to hire talented people who are more like a decathlete than a single-sport virtuoso, because the former can adapt and change more effectively.

The Benefits

Flexibility is the principal reason to hire that decathlete. The rate of change is increasing every day. What you master today could be obsolete tomorrow. By having a willingness to learn other skills, your team has a much higher possibility of adapting to new market conditions.

Team members who learn other skills make their area of mastery that much stronger. Often you can learn from fields that are complementary. This applies to all service professional fields.

Finally, from a business perspective, mastering many skills helps people understand the abilities of others within the firm. When one member gains insight into their colleagues' abilities, that person is better able to provide referrals, thus making the firm stronger as a whole.

(33)
Give Back

Strengthen Your Community

Your firm serves people. People are members of various communities that come in many variations. One might be a local or national organization. It could be a professional, informal, faith-based, or public organization. It might be physical or virtual. The common ground is that these communities of people use the services or products of your firm. Since they support you, the right thing to do is to strengthen them by giving back.

Benefits of Giving Back

- First, you benefit from the deep, personal satisfaction you gain from helping people improve or change their lives.

- Second, a stronger community can focus on growth that in turn opens new possibilities for your professional endeavors.

- Third, since you are perceived as a leader in your community, people want to work with you.

- Last, your firm, as a team, comes closer together. The best giving is collaborative, offering the opportunity to be thankful together.

Ways to Give Back

TIME: Volunteering can range from helping at a weekend soup kitchen to a longer commitment to an organization by joining their board.

TALENT: Everyone has a skill. Most not-for-profits cannot afford your skills. By donating to them, you significantly expand their ability to help others.

TREASURE: Invest your hard-earned money back into the community. Pick a passion and purpose, and back it.

TRANSACTIONS: People buy products and services. Make one that is better, smarter, and sustainable.

Give as You Go

I recommend "giving as you go." Do not wait until you are old or hit some magic number in your bank account. Your communities need you now. The key is to determine the best way you can give, and then get started. You will be thankful. The best thing about giving is that you always get more than you give.

Take a Look:

Pay It Forward

I am a champion of architectural and design students learning from practitioners as well as from books. To help students gain access to the real world, I helped conceive, establish, and support a Visiting Critic Chair in the Architectural Department at Cornell by investing my time, talent, and money.

I did this in part because of an architect named Henry Hill who visited the school during my student days. He helped me understand that architecture is far more than attractive drawings; that it is a complex business with many facets. Hill became one of my first mentors. He gave his time and talent. I was pleased to follow his example for the next generation.

Strategy

Stop Chasing Fads and Build Enduring Principles

Build a Brand, Not a Style

Styles and fads come and go. Brands built on principles endure. If you want to scale your business, you need to build a principle-driven brand, not a style. Brands represent a set of values that serve clients over time. Fads and styles serve a limited number of clients for a limited period of time. Building a brand means focusing your energies on establishing trust with clients. Trust signals that you are client-focused, consistent in quality, and exceptional at service.

Method Matters

As you build your firm, you want to be known for your method of value creation. This applies to both product and service companies. The better, smarter, and more effective you are at creating value, the stronger your venture will grow. If you focus only on style, you are in a weak position if your style becomes unfashionable.

Look at Me vs. Being in the Background

While brand is more important than style, I want to make clear that design matters. Design has the power to transform space, products, and services into an exceptional and memorable experience. When you singularly concentrate on "look at me" projects, you will be challenged to remain viable in the marketplace.

In the world of architecture and design, the limiting factor for most firms is the desire to have every single project or product publicly acknowledged. I do recognize that everyone enjoys the feeling of having highly visible projects and products. If a signature project is what a client wants and needs, then you deliver it. However, less celebrated "background" projects are equally important. While you should always bring your best to any project, background projects can be opportunities for innovation and more subtle integration of style and design elements.

Always Listen

In trying to make every product or project famous, you are putting your ego before your clients' needs. It is risky because once your clients realize that you have stopped listening to them, they will go elsewhere. The key to having both a great brand and style is to always listen to the client.

Listening carefully to your client establishes the trust needed to blaze ahead or to explore new possibilities. It helps you understand when a product or project is considered a showcase endeavor or when it is time to be boldly in the background while sticking to your quality standards.

Slow Business Growth

Take the Long View

We live in the age of the instant billionaire. While a handful of young Silicon Valley entrepreneurs have burst onto the scene with spectacular multibillion-dollar buyouts and public offerings that shock us, they are the exception. Building a successful service firm is a slow and steady journey. It requires taking the long-term view.

Hour by Hour

When you boil it down, service firms sell hours. You might bundle them up or break them out for your clients on their invoice, but in the end, you measure your return on the number of hours you can profitably bill. The key to expanding is to grow the number of billable hours.

On occasion, service professionals get lured into trying to take a shortcut to quicker money. For example, perhaps an attorney is offered equity in a hot tech deal. It could be that an architect is encouraged to become a real estate developer. Maybe a product designer is asked to waive the fees for a piece of the product royalties.

"We neither shun growth nor idolize it. We view it as a by-product of achieving our other goals."

— McKINSEY & COMPANY

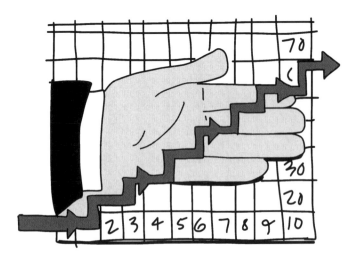

While you should always evaluate opportunities to generate revenues, service firms become successful one hour at a time. Keep your focus on the target.

Quality, Then Quantity

The only way to gain billable hours is to deliver consistent value to your clients. When you are starting out, you must focus on the quality of your work versus the quantity of billed hours. Quality work can be done at any price point. It can be delivered for low-cost projects as well as showcase projects. What's important is that your clients see that they received value for their money. For you, it is necessary to deliver that quality in a profitable manner. Once you do that, you provide the opportunity for more client referrals. These referrals pave the way for expanding the amount of business you win.

Compounding Effect

Service firms that concentrate on steadily providing quality work will benefit from the effects of compounding. The first compounding effect is the rise in repeat business. Who doesn't love repeat business? It is less expensive to win and helps you better understand your client's needs. The more you understand your clients, the harder it is for others to compete against you. The second compounding effect is that satisfied clients generate leads for you.

Stretching Yourself and Your Client
When I think about growth with a client, I often think of the properties of a rubber band. You want to collaborate with your client and grow together over time. Sometimes your client will stretch you; sometimes you will stretch them. Often a client has an idea of what they want, but you feel you have a better solution. Sharing your approach is fine, but be careful not to push the client too hard; to where they become uncomfortable dealing with you. In other words, don't stretch them to the point where they lose their trust in you and the relationship breaks.

The stretching needs to be done slowly. When you stretch a rubber band slowly, you know when you have reached the farthest it will go without breaking. Similarly, avoid stretching the client too far or too fast. With shared purpose, you can move forward to a new, higher level. When you go too far or too fast, you can break the rubber band or break the relationship. You and your clients should look for ways to stretch each other. That is how the best value is created for everyone and a trusted advisor relationship is formed.

(36)
Don't Be First

Be the Best, Not the First

I embrace the new, the unique, and the innovative. The new offers the prospect for growth. New tools can help drive down costs and even spark the creation of new products and services. While I love the new, I prefer to be the best rather than the first.

Look Before You Leap

You may face tremendous pressure to sink time and cash into a new technology, rush into a recently opened marketplace, or implement a new management technique. I suggest you take a step back before leaping into anything new.

New products and services are usually accompanied by unanticipated problems that drain your cash, your energy, and your focus from winning new business and delivering quality to your current customers. While you don't want to be first, you also don't want to be last. Plan to be a swift second.

Be a Swift Second

The key to being a swift second is to pay attention to new ideas or improvements. Formal and informal surveys and beta testing can help you determine whether the new ideas are simply hype or are maturing into a viable option for you. If a new idea appears to be viable, then be prepared to use it. If you recognize it as hype or a flawed product or service, you will have avoided the financial pain and kept your firm in a healthy position.

Even if the improvement does merit investment, you still have to take some risk. A zero-risk option means you avoid being first, but you might well end up last. To avoid being last, gain an understanding of the new idea and how it could make significant improvements to your organization.

Take a Look:

Watch, Wait, Adapt

In my world, I have been a second-mover on software systems. This position has served us well for 50 years. When CAD (Computer Aided Drafting) first showed up, many firms moved quickly to use it. Even some architectural firms ventured into CAD, although no clear standard existed. Millions of dollars and countless hours were invested in making their own CAD systems.

While our competitors did this, we focused on winning business and providing high-quality results to our clients. Once we saw that the first wave of problems had been fixed and the initial prices for CAD systems dropped, we stepped in and saved millions. We watched, waited, and then adapted. When we saw the standards taking root and the kinks worked out, we migrated to the industry standard.

We have been committed to, invested in, and taken full advantage of this tool ever since, constantly investing in upgrades when appropriate.

Open New Markets or Services with a Project

Open with a Project

Entering a new market is risky business. I see many companies rent offices, hire staff, and set up full shop before they have any business in the door. This is both expensive and speculative. In other words, it's dangerous.

The smarter way to enter a marketplace is with a project

already in hand; for example, either a new location or a new service for your organization. The project should be both profitable and big enough to give you presence in the new market for a period of time. If it is a smaller and short-term assignment, be selective. Make sure it is a significant or noteworthy project and positions you to explore the potential of the greater marketplace.

Growth with Your Clients

The ideal situation is when your clients bring you with them into new marketplaces. Exploring new markets together occurs when trust has been built by your performance for them in other markets. Excel in one location and they will ask you to join them in others. If you have strong working relationships, you should inquire about where they are expanding and looking for opportunities.

Land and Expand

Once you make solid progress with your initial project in a new location, tune into the community and find where you can offer a similar service. Engage in conversations to explore where you can create value or offer a new service to the market.

It is from this exploration that you generate new clients. When you win another piece of serious business, you can officially claim the territory and expand into the new marketplace. You minimize the risk, build a solid reputation based on a local project, and generate revenues that keep the firm healthy and sustained. It will take time, but slow and steady wins the race when building a service firm with multiple locations offering multiple services.

New Services

One or a few people in your organization might have an idea for a new service or product. They work on it with little or no firm support. For new services, we often enter them through a "skunk works" approach. We try to support champions who are really passionate about a service we currently do not provide. Once they have proof of concept and a successful project or two, we then consider offering that service to the market.

Take a Look:

Grow with a Strong Client

We did some great work for a multinational investment bank. At one point, they asked us to identify a
firm in the UK that could help set up their offices in
London. Since we did not have an operation in the
UK, we dutifully worked to generate a list of excellent organizations. Using our list, they did their own
research, but were not excited by any of our suggestions. They came back to ask us if we would open up
a UK office and do the work. We signed a contract,
and that is how we entered the UK marketplace. You
should always look for a strong client to grow with in
a new market.

Sleep on Questions

Urgency Everywhere

As I've said, it seems like the pace of change gets faster with each year I have been in business. Everyone operates in an urgent and nanosecond response mode. Yes, sometimes you need to make a swift decision, but most of the time you can take a moment to reflect on it. Nothing could be worse than rushing a decision and then suffering the consequences of a bad choice.

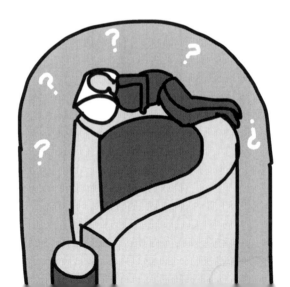

Reputation and Responsibility

In the service profession, your brand is built on your reputation for delivering value. Good decision-making consistently generates value. It is crucial to invest quality time into making solid choices.

As a business owner, you have the responsibility to manage the risks you take for the firm. This includes venturing into new markets, quoting fees on potentially significant, higher-reward projects, or buying into new operating or financial systems. Do not rush any of these sizable decisions.

Sleep on It

The solution is simple. When you are faced with a complex issue or presented with a challenging request from a client, before you race into any decision, mull it over. This is especially important when a client presents a particularly challenging request. Never say no immediately. You want to keep the client happy, but you also need to be able to deliver the project in a profitable yet timely way.

Ask clients for a day to think about it, and tell them you will get back to them. This gives you the time to consider alternative possibilities to achieve the desired outcome. Whether they are a client, an employee, or a friend, be certain to respond back.

Not making a hasty decision applies to internal situations as well. Key hires, buying into major systems, and taking on additional space are all issues for which you must exercise great care.

Deliver on Your Promises
Sleeping on an issue supplies you with the power to deliver your response with confidence. From this uninterrupted concentration, you've been able to weigh the advantages and disadvantages, and generate some alternative scenarios. With this greater sense of clarity, you can make a commitment and deliver on your promise to your teammates and your clients.

Missed Boats
Yes, you will miss some business by requesting time to think about it. This is okay. It's far better than to say yes, make a terrible decision, and sink your own firm as a result. More opportunities will always arise for you to pursue. It is better to thrive another day to win them.

Explore Unknown Territory

Charting Your Course

If you are just starting a service firm, it is important to master your part of the market. You want to be the best at what you do and be known as the go-to professional services firm for that niche. I suggest you also invest time in exploring unknown territories. Exploration expands your horizon. One of its benefits is that it gives you time to redirect your resources and chart a new path that leads to sustained growth.

Benefits to Exploring Unknown Territory

AVOID BEING A SLAVE TO SEASONAL BUSINESS:
Some service companies collect the majority of their
fees in a small, defined season. This is true with tax
professionals who have a massive inflow of business in
the spring, followed by a trickle throughout the rest of
the year.

As a business owner and leader, if you are pegged to
seasonal sales, you are at the mercy of a feast-or-famine
cycle. With a bountiful year, your firm keeps growing.
If you experience famine, you may have to lay off some
people and will struggle to make it to the next season.
Look to find sectors that have complementary seasons
for your firm. This will help you balance out your cash
flow and build up a reserve.

FREE YOURSELF FROM BUSINESS CYCLES: The health
of your professional services firm is directly linked to the
health of your clients. If your clients are a single industry,
you face riding a single business cycle along with them,
putting your firm at risk. Some firms mature and eventually decline. Others accept the cycles and emerge as
strong players. If your firm explores unknown territories,
you are likely to tune into new trends, spot disruptive
players, and win them over as new clients. As a trend

spotter, you can also help your current mature clients adapt and adjust to the new realities. You create value for them so that you both stay in business.

WATCH OUT FOR SHOCKS: Massive shocks can dramatically change your commercial reality. Terrorist acts occur, greed creates bubbles, and political landscapes experience sweeping changes. Any of these can wipe out your firm if you are limited in your scope. Being in diverse markets and geographies and gaining scale help to maximize your ability to endure tough times. Remember, being organized and comfortable doing both large and small projects profitably can get you through the hard times.

Where to Explore

For professional services firms, here are three ways to search unknown territories:

- Explore new client types.
- Explore new services for your current clients.
- Explore new geographic markets.

Operations

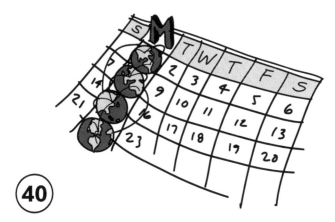

(40)

Monday Morning Call

Monday Wake-up Call

Make Mondays matter. Start your week with a Monday wake-up call to your leadership team. It is unfashionable these days to recommend meetings. Most people see them as a waste of time. Poorly run meetings are in fact a waste of time, and I hate wasting time. Let's be clear— the old adage that time is money is 100 percent true in my business.

The key is to have a well-designed meeting. If you do it right, the Monday Call sets the direction, pace, and tone for a successful week. The essential question is: What is the blueprint of a valuable call and what are its benefits?

Be There.
No Excuses.

Five Benefits of a Monday Call

COMMITMENT: Always attend the call unless you or your next of kin is deathly sick. If you want to be a successful leader, it starts with commitment. For the past 50 years, our leaders committed to the Monday Call. They defend that time and bring their full attention to it.

TALK: Information is the lifeblood of business. Keep it flowing. It helps you pick up on new clients, share innovations, and spot rising problems that need to be addressed. It prevents information hoarding, breaks down silos, and means greater prospects for collaboration.

BUILD TRUST: Trust is everything. It is built by having a consistent conversation. Our Monday Calls share vital information. Leaders are then able to open up new conversations off-line that help one another win new business or think through problems for solutions.

GROWTH: Share growth opportunities. At Gensler, we focus on real business prospects—those that are in progress or are concrete, including near-term prospects that need teamwork to convert into clients. We avoid unrealistic prospecting. When you share victories or near-term prospects, you build momentum. Leaders become motivated to grow the firm's book of business.

FACE CHALLENGES: Every business experiences challenges. Face them. Losses and problems can be managed so they don't spin out of control. When we work through a problem, everyone can learn from it. Over the past 50 years, this culture of facing challenges has built an institutional memory at Gensler. It helps us spot potential problems early on and avoid them whenever and wherever possible. Have the courage to face challenges as a group. No finger-pointing. It is not helpful.

Three Elements of a Great Monday Meeting

BE RELIGIOUS ABOUT IT: The call matters. Be there. No excuses.

PREPARE: Being prepared is a matter of respect for yourself and others. However it works for you as an individual, make sure you have thought about the possibilities and problems at hand. Prioritize them. Bring the most important ones forward for your fellow leaders to help advance or fix.

DOCUMENT AND SHARE: Elect someone to document the Monday Call's invaluable information. Once documented, it should be circulated within the day. This keeps everyone informed and the conversation going off-line. The Monday Call notes might help spark new ideas or fresh fixes for a problem.

It's Friday, Count the Cash

A business is comprised of individuals who need to pay their bills, buy homes, and send their kids to college. To do that, you need cash—not the kind that will arrive one day, but the kind that is in the bank today.

In the design and architectural world, most professionals are uncomfortable discussing money. Few, if any, architect or design schools integrate basic business classes into their curriculum. The same is true for many other service professional schools. The result is a world filled with talented people struggling to survive. Regardless of your service sector, it is essential to get smart about money.

Years ago, I attended a meeting that introduced a common sense approach to this issue: count the cash in the bank on Friday night. We have been doing this now for 50 consecutive profitable years. Here are some of the benefits of counting the cash in the bank on Friday:

EVERYONE IS AN OWNER: Owners take responsibility for their results. Whether the results are good or bad, owners know where they stand and can take action to make improvements. By counting the cash on Friday, you can see the results of your work. If you create value, clients will compensate you fairly. You can wake up the next day and do it all over again.

BUILD REAL BUSINESS: Friday tells you whether you have real clients or not. Unfortunately, many clients have great ideas but no money to pay you. Research them before you start work. The world of design and architecture is packed with prestigious design competitions offering minimal or no cash rewards. Worse are reverse auctions, where they pit firms against each other for a "race to the bottom." If you do free work, even if you win the competition, you lose the race. Without cash, you cannot pay your expenses, and that means failure sooner or later. Keep your attention on winning real business from real clients.

NO-BORROW RULE: We believe in a no-borrow rule. This originated from my experience as a young architect, where one of my original bosses ran his firm into the ground. He kept borrowing from the bank to fund future receivables. When those receivables failed to materialize, he was left with enormous debt and no way to pay the bills. As nice and talented as he was as an architect, he was a disaster as a businessman. I committed to avoid borrowing, and made sure that wherever I worked or created was as concentrated on delivering a great design service as it was on being financially healthy.

EVERYONE IS A COLLECTOR: Most designers, architects, or service professionals turn up their noses at the collection process. In fact, most see it as beneath them. They pass collections off to a dedicated collector. I don't believe in that model at all. If a client asks you to bring your best to the table and you deliver, you need to be compensated in a fair and timely manner.

If you are a service professional, you are the one delivering value. You are in the most powerful position to make sure that the payment is delivered. If you work closely with the client and understand their enterprise, you have the highest possibility of understanding your client's financial health.

If you don't know about your client's ability to pay you, then you can't be sure that you have a viable client. We have always and will always focus on the ones who pay. It is critical that your firm is healthy so you can continue to attract the best talent and incorporate the latest tools of your trade. If you operate from paycheck to paycheck, you will be unable to make a difference for your client. This is why in our firm, we who originate the project and do the work must also make sure that we are paid. By being empowered to collect, it creates a firm of owners who can grow successfully year after year.

Pay Your Bills
Just as you need to collect on your bills, your consultants, vendors, and service providers also need to collect on their bills. If you pay them promptly, they will continue to give you the quality service you deserve and expect.

(42)

Know Your
Numbers

Be Number-Smart

Different industries demand different skills, yet there is
one skill required of any professional in any industry—
that is to be number-smart. In fact, I would argue that
everyone at every level of your organization should be
solidly numerate. The better people understand numbers,
the more likely they will be able to build a strong, sustainable business. Profit is the lifeblood of your business.

If you and your team are solid with numbers, you will understand how your daily decisions add up to produce either a healthy business or a sick and dying one.

Make Smart Commitments

Every day you are doing deals big and small. You might have in-house purchasing decisions or proposals to develop with the right fee to win new business. By understanding the numbers, you can make smart commitments that make your firm healthier and stronger.

Know Your Final Number

Over and over again, I see firms make commitments they cannot keep. It drives me crazy. They put together proposals set up to fail. They underprice their proposals and then put everyone in an untenable position. Projects in jeopardy threaten their firm's survival and alienate their clients. To avoid this catastrophe, know your final number. You must understand and communicate what it takes to meet your clients' needs in a way that is profitable to you.

Know Your Marketplace Numbers

While your final numbers matter, what matters even more is your marketplace's numbers. If you are consistently rejected when you go to close a deal, then you need to look inward. Have you hit the ceiling of what your client is willing to pay if you are a premium brand? Do you need to innovate and offer new and highly valuable services? Have you lived up to your promised standards, or are your clients unhappy with their level of service from you?

Lessons Learned from Losing

When you lose a bid, don't agonize over it. Learn from it. Ask who won and why. Try to understand what made the difference. The more intelligence you gather, the smarter you will become and the sooner you can figure out how best to serve the prospective client. You might also identify whether your niche is having its profit squeezed out of existence. By being number savvy, you can recognize the trend and be better positioned to direct your leadership efforts toward new niches and fresh opportunities.

Take a Look:

Keep Good Records

First, you need to figure out what it will cost you to do a project. It is important to understand what other competitors are charging and what services they are providing. Quality or service differences may exist, but you must know what the marketplace is for your service. Determine whether you are going to be a low-, medium-, or high-priced provider commensurate with both the quality and quantity of the offer.

Second, keep accurate records of what a similar project cost you before. Once I was working with one of our talented project managers who kept very detailed records on his projects. When we were asked to design a 200,000-square-foot office building, he researched his files to determine what a similar past project had cost to complete.

He showed me a detailed analysis and then adjusted for inflation. When he proposed a price we should quote, I asked him what the going market price was for these services. He had worked up an offer that was 50 percent higher than the going rate. At that spread, we were clearly not going to get the assignment. I asked him to review what we had done in the past and to think about a new way to go about it.

When he figured it out, we were able to offer a competitive fee. In the end, we were rewarded with three things: a happy client, a profitable project, and a new approach to providing the appropriate solution.

43

No Silos

A silo group is a self-supporting office, studio, or unit that may or may not share firm-wide support, but basically operates by developing its own business, is responsible for its own costs, and retains the bulk of its profits. It is basically an autonomous entity.

Get Rid of Silo Thinking

When building your business, make the commitment to eliminate silo thinking from day one. Silo thinking interferes with the flow of information, sets groups on collision courses with each other, and slows down your company's ability to best serve its clients. Silo thinking encourages more divisions, departments, and practice groups unless you work hard to defeat it.

Let the information flow.

The problem is not with creating strong practice groups within your service firm or with having back-office divisions. You need specialization as you scale up your venture. The problem is that silo thinking usually creeps into your company's culture. There is an alternative.

Collaborative Culture

As you know, I am a champion of the one-firm firm culture (see Chapter 7, *One-Firm Firm*). It is about building a family culture that is rich in trust, high in collaboration, and deeply committed to building a single brand.

Living by this collaborative culture on a daily basis is important for the employees as well as the leadership teams. Sharing people among groups gives your staff the opportunity to expand and balance workloads. Open-book management, sharing the cost and profits, multi-group projects, and a strong internal referral market fuel the kind of cooperation and communication that keep silo thinking from taking root.

The Benefits of Collaboration

The advantage of collaboration is that it frees the flow of information and willingness to find common ground with other internal groups. It also helps remove the "eat what you kill" mentality.

You will waste time determining who gets credit for a piece of business. When everyone shares in the success, everyone feels part of the organization and the total firm wins. If your employees feel they get credit only for specific jobs they do, they will attempt assignments that might be better done by others. If they feel they get no reward or recognition for exposing their clients to other services or locations, then the leverage of a one-firm firm is lost.

When information is free-flowing, new project opportunities find the right home, troubleshooting resolves a client's problem faster, and vital know-how circulates throughout the organization. Collaboration helps find internal hot spots as well. You cannot avoid friction; however, if you have a collaborative culture, problems will surface sooner and give leadership teams the ability to fix them before things get out of control.

Collaboration ultimately advances the virtuous cycle with your client. The easier it is to work with talent across your organization, the more your client will direct business to you. The more business you generate, the stronger you grow and the more services you bring to market.

No Territory Control

The Problems of Control

When firms grow, one of the first things they do is split into silos and divide market territories. When they then assign people to control the territories, fiefdoms result. I think this is entirely the wrong way to grow a service firm. Three major problems appear with this approach:

- Infighting often occurs. People argue over how to split revenues when clients migrate from one group to another. This happens when a client expands geographically or into new product lines that need to be serviced by different parts of the organization. Infighting often results in your clients being under-served. When your clients lose and walk away, you lose, too.

- Often you are competing against yourself. I have seen different groups at the same firm submit bids to win the same client, sending a signal that you are not coordinated. This erodes your long-term profitability, as each group races to the bottom to win the client.

- Finally, when you encourage territorial control, you miss the power of an internal referral marketplace.

The Benefits of Soft Control
Breaking down the territorial control model benefits your organization.

- First, you dramatically open up the possibilities for people to share contacts and leads. When people know they are part of a family culture, they work hard to help each other. More eyes and ears are open and on the lookout for opportunities (see Chapter 40, *Monday Morning Call*).

- Second, you develop an ownership mentality around your company's brand throughout the firm. People want the brand to succeed, so they are motivated to generate leads and share them with their fellow brand champions.

- Third, sharing leads encourages willingness to collaborate. By eliminating silos and territory control, talent can move around internally to where they are most needed to best serve the client. Increased mobility is exciting for service professionals who are looking to expand their horizons into challenging projects. This is beneficial for clients because they receive the best possible talent from your firm for their project.

- Finally, by sharing clients and working collaboratively, you build trust. Your team sees that the internal referral market works. Sometimes you generate more leads than you receive, while other times you receive more than you generate. Over time, it levels out.

If the internal referral marketplace is working well, then your team begins to move away from trying just to maximize its own short-term gains toward seeing how to help the firm reach its best potential over the long run. Support this approach when you determine bonuses and compensation. In order to successfully achieve no territorial control, compensate everybody out of the same pool.

Clients stand to gain when there's potential for additional bundled services. In such a case, clients are exposed to more than a single group of skilled professionals. The key to making this model work is to integrate the no-territory approach with a strong and clear leadership team that guides the region and practices. This helps navigate conflicts when they arise and activates possible new collaborations.

Start to Finish

Power of Ownership

I own it; therefore, it owns me. I believe in the power of ownership to produce better and faster results. Responsibility and commitment to quality are inherent to being an owner. Owners know they live or die commercially by how well they serve their employees and their clients. That is why I advise businesses in the service field to have a start-to-finish approach toward serving clients.

Playing Hot Potato

Today, businesses generally divide the value chain. The basic model involves sending in the sales team to a potential client, following up with the production team, and then wrapping up with the billing and collections department. I think this formula is a disaster in the professional services world. It pits everyone against each other internally, and the blame game begins when the work doesn't go as expected.

If you don't start a project correctly, you can never complete it correctly.

Start to Finish

A better way is to have your employees and teams own their client's project from start to finish. The team does the pitch to win the business, works to produce and deliver it, and makes the call to get paid fairly and in a timely fashion. It is wise to remember that if you don't finish a project correctly, you can lose everything. It's the last two percent of a job that ensures your successful completion of the project.

When you make the pitch, you know exactly what you promise the client. You will deliver on the promise in a way that is mutually beneficial and avoids over-promising, under-delivering, or delivering at a loss. The client buys into a brand and into you when you make the pitch. You establish the trust required to work through a project together. That is why it is essential that the same team who pitches the deal also delivers the deal.

Most people complain about collections. Service professionals think it is beneath them or a hassle. However, I think it is important for the team to acknowledge that their compensation is linked to getting paid by the client. By doing collections themselves, they learn whether they have a real client or not. By concentrating on real and reliable clients, the team has the highest chances of long-term success.

Winning Business

(46)

Everyone
Is a Marketer

Empower Everyone to Win

If you want to build a business that constantly grows,
every person in your firm must be empowered to win
business. Remember, when you try to sell something,
learn to ask for the sale. I am serious about everyone's
responsibility to grow the business. You are a family and
you have to take care of each other.

Separation Blues

Most businesses today have separate departments for
sales, production, and collections. This is a recipe for

staying small and missing growth opportunities. However, in the long term, this approach will lead to being out-maneuvered by your competitors.

Separate departments can also lead to unnecessary conflict. Sales might overpromise, producers might forget to mention new, valuable features, and everyone can get in a bind over pricing, timing, and payment.

My alternative has worked for me since the beginning: everyone on the team is a generator of possibilities for the firm by developing selling, marketing, and collections skills.

Expertise Closes Deals

As an expert in your business, you are the right person to determine what it would take to deliver on your prospective client's needs. It also means you understand what it takes to deliver on that need. You, the expert, are then in the best possible place to scope and price the work.

Collections Keeps It Real

Most professionals have never had to collect a payment. Payment collection is an important skill. When you do so, you discover a few things right away.

Learn to ask for the sale.

- First, is this a good client or a deadbeat?

- Second, you confirm the value you created. When you produce great work, you should be confident asking to be fairly compensated for it.

- Third, you understand the financial health of your firm. Managing costs and cash received means your firm will have a healthy business.

Three Ways to Come Together

LEARN TO LISTEN: Stay tuned. Listen to what is happening around you and dial into the small details that might lead to potential clients and projects. Over the years, the team I worked with attended events, expos, dinners, lectures, and meet-ups with clients. By asking good questions and then listening, you can discover unanticipated selling opportunities.

LEARN TO SHARE: If you meet a prospect, it is important to understand your firm well enough and to have enough social capital and good will to become skilled at sharing potential leads. Direct the prospect to the right expert so that your organization can meet the client's needs. Act as a family. As you share leads, others will do the same.

LEARN THE TOOLS: If you want everyone to be empowered, you need to give them access to excellent tools and support. The latter might include people who are talented at developing proposals or planning compelling presentations.

One other tool is a set of filters that aids the team in knowing the size of the contract they can negotiate before calling in a more senior member of the firm. This helps manage risk and keeps you growing. An example of a filter would be dollar limitations for contract signing given to each managing individual. Some may have a $10,000 limit, others may have a $50,000 limit, depending on their experience and level of responsibility. Create your own filters appropriate for your organization.

Win Real Business

If you are serious about running your own professional services firm, you need to be resolute about winning real business. When the company wins, everyone wins—projects you can deliver with a profit. I am talking about contracts that put cash in your bank account. Charge appropriately for your services, but deliver beyond the client's expectations.

Beware of Fool's Gold

Service professionals are constantly being lured into traps by the promise of fool's gold. These offers look good at first, but upon inspection will bleed you dry and run you out of business.

Listed below are three common traps to avoid.

NON-CASH OR LOW-CASH PRIZE COMPETITIONS: This trap is particularly popular in the design world. The promise is always the same: the winner of the prize gains prestige and visibility, and with these you can attract business. While some competitions may do this, most do nothing more than take up your precious time. Remember, in a service profession, time really is money.

"SHOW ME WHAT WE SHOULD DO": When a client wants free solutions to their problems, they are asking you to share your intellectual property for no compensation. The worst part of this approach is that you are providing a solution before you understand the client's problem in detail.

REVERSE AUCTIONS: Big companies invite firms to participate in a "race to the bottom." The lure of winning future contracts for a big brand-name company and the chance to showcase the big brand as a client in marketing materials attract many firms to join in. It never works out well. The big brands now focus on you as a discount provider rather than a value creator. Your margins are permanently squeezed. Chasing reverse auctions puts your firm at financial risk because it takes an investment of time and resources to prepare pitches. These are unbilled hours that are nonrecoverable unless you win. Chase enough of these and you will be out of business in no time (see also Chapter 54, *People Value What They Pay For*).

In the end, even the client loses. Professional services are not a commodity and are rarely used to solve generic problems. The best way to serve clients is to engage in a dialogue, become a trusted advisor, and then create offerings and solutions customized to meet their needs. This approach will be rewarding to all parties.

Unanticipated Opportunities

Welcome Luck

Luck is not a strategy, but when it comes your way, act on it. The question is how to stumble upon unanticipated opportunities and what to do once they show up in your life.

Always Be Curious

Be ready to take advantage of luck when it happens. I believe the building block of all luck is curiosity. If you are curious about the world around you and explore it, you will bump into all kinds of people, places, and possibilities. The stronger your curiosity, the more unanticipated opportunities you will discover.

Explore the New and Familiar
Exploration is the step following curiosity. It means venturing into new areas and taking a fresh look at the familiar. Perhaps you accept an invitation to speak at a conference in a field that is just starting to emerge, or perhaps you engage in a stimulating conversation with a stranger during a commercial flight or chance meeting at a party. By exploring and asking questions, you will encounter unanticipated opportunities.

Act on It
Luck is beneficial only when you act on it. If you encounter an opportunity in an unanticipated circumstance, engage it. Turn your mind on to the possibilities. I have always said, "I would rather be lucky than smart." But if you are lucky, you must be smart enough to welcome it and respond to it.

Take a Look:

Act on Serendipity

When I was running late in a meeting in NYC, I called my assistant to rearrange my flight schedule. She called back to say she refused to make the flight arrangements because United would charge $1,000 to change my ticket. Being cheap (and cautious with our firm's money), I told her about a new airline, JetBlue, that had cheap flights to San Francisco for $115.

She argued that they had only coach seats and that I didn't fit very well in a coach seat (I'm a big person). But for the difference in cost, I finally convinced her to get me a seat on JetBlue's later flight.

As I was settling into my seat, just before the plane pushed back, a man's voice came on the PA system saying he was David Neeleman, the founder and CEO of JetBlue, and would be joining the flight attendants to give out drinks and Blue chips, and that he hoped to talk to all the passengers. A little later in the flight, he reached my seat, showed me it was not adjusted properly, and then asked what I did. "I'm an architect," I said, adding, "we do airports."

He replied, "I'm trying to build a new terminal at JFK and am not happy with the architect the Port Authority suggested." We exchanged business cards, and two weeks later I received an RFP for the terminal project. Three weeks later, JetBlue selected Gensler as the architect. What an unanticipated opportunity!

No Project Too Small for a Great Client

Stop Being Arrogant

Many service companies refuse smaller projects. They do this to even the biggest and most respected firms. Their attitude is that small projects are unworthy of their time or talents. I think this is both arrogant and a missed opportunity to serve great clients.

No Project Too Small for a Great Client

I say there is no such thing as a little project or an insignificant client. Each project you accept for a client is an opportunity to showcase your ability to deliver value and quality. Small projects might not be glamorous or even fun, but they are important. Small projects can be the starting point of a relationship with a potential new client, or they might be part of nurturing a current valuable client. Either way, they are vital to building your business. You are in the business of servicing your clients—service them!

The benefits of doing small projects are trust, growth, and resilience.

TRUST-BUILDING: Delivering on a small project with the same level of excellence and enthusiasm you bring to a big project establishes trust. It builds trust in both directions when you deliver the small project in a way that brings value to the client and remains profitable to you. This helps both parties recognize there's real value in working together.

GROWTH OPPORTUNITIES: Great clients bring growth opportunities, such as exploring new products or services or expanding into new geographies. If they call upon you to help them figure out how to explore those new possibilities, you can grow with them. Also, by doing small projects well, you will be first in line for consideration when bigger projects become available.

RESILIENCE: Markets go up and down. If you have a narrow focus and limited experience working with constrained client budgets or smaller projects, you are likely to be driven out of business when times are tough. Knowing how to create value during difficult times makes you resilient. It allows you to keep serving clients and generate cash. Cash is vital if you want to weather the tough periods until a time of plenty returns.

Take a Look:

The Little Ones Count

The chairman of the board of Levi Strauss called me after a developer friend referred me. He asked if I could help find the proper finish on a wood deck he had built at his summer home. Apparently, none of the finishes he had seen so far were acceptable to his wife and him. I did some research and found a suitable solution.

From that contact, he later asked us to do the interior of their 600,000-square-foot headquarters and two buildings in the complex. Not a bad trade-off for a few hours of research!

Get to the Table

How to Win Real Clients

The path to winning a portfolio of real clients is paved with the answer "no." Many young professionals who are technically skilled lack an understanding of how to build a book of business. They have zero sales skills and have no idea how to get to the table and close the deal. Four basic steps lead to growing a profitable business:

EXPLORE AND LISTEN: Business rarely falls into your lap. You must go out, explore, and find clients. You must generate opportunities and be ready for unanticipated ones. Once you find a prospective client, you must quickly switch gears into deep listening mode. Ask good questions and seek to understand where the client is strong and where they are seeking help. Listen for the smallest cues that could indicate the potential for collaboration.

GET TO THE TABLE: Once you have a solid understanding of the client, open it up to a dialogue. At this point, return to being an explorer. Broaden your exchange with the prospect. Put forward some "what-if" scenarios and share some of your firm's experiences that showcase its value. Your mission is to understand your prospective client's needs and figure out how you and your firm can contribute value to them.

Once you understand their needs, it is important that you sit across the table from an empowered manager who can make a purchasing decision. If that individual is unable to control the selection, then enlist your original contact to be your advocate. Have that contact guide you to the right person who can make the decision.

At this point, you will need to return to the exploring and listening stages again to build a complete picture and to find out the best way to present a proposal to the client. You would be amazed at how many professionals are uncomfortable with or dislike this process. You must instill—in both your team and your firm—the confidence and commitment to ask questions. Always remember to ask your prospect for their business and the opportunity to work with them.

AT THE TABLE: Before you have won your spot at the table to present a proposal, make sure you understand the bidding process. You want to show them respect and position yourself for a win. Your proposal should create value for them, and at the same time be profitable to you. A "win at any cost" approach will destroy your firm. Change the discussion from cost to value.

Just as you respect your client, you need to respect yourself and the value you create. Make a win-win deal at the table. If you end up on the losing side, then you did not have the appropriate credentials or personal chemistry to win the project.

STAY AT THE TABLE: Then comes the moment of truth, always. You get a yes or a no on your proposal. The yes is exciting, while the no defeats most professionals. They hear the no, walk away from the table, and are never heard from again.

This is the wrong approach. The first thing to do is understand why you did not win. Place a congenial call to the client to ask if they might provide helpful feedback on why they chose another firm. Learn from it. Often, the door is not completely closed. They might want to work with you, but have certain constraints. This is when you can adjust your offer, your fee, your schedule, or the chemistry of your team with their team; still make it profitable; and deliver value to the prospect. They may have had a previous relationship with your competitor. Your goal is to stay at the table. "No" doesn't always mean no.

If you do not win this second attempt, try to "stay at the table" by maintaining the relationship. This keeps the conversation going and alerts you to other needs they might have in the future. By staying at the table, you are ready to pitch again and go for the close.

The only tables you should walk away from are the ones that constantly demand free work and endanger your firm. At all the rest, keep a seat so that you can find ways to create value in the future.

Respect Your Clients

Show Them Respect

Your clients don't care how much you know until they know how much you care. An old adage in the design world goes something like this: "I could do great work if only I did not have to deal with a client."

Many service providers get caught up in trying to show the client how outstanding they are at what they do. They end up monopolizing the limelight and squeezing the life out of their client's ability to explain the problem at hand. This is downright dumb. Show your clients respect. They are smart. They have built businesses. If they are calling you in to help solve a problem, use that as your starting point. Listen to them. Try to understand what they truly need. After that, you can share your stories and case studies to resolve their particular issue.

Speak Their Language

It drives me crazy when service providers drown their clients in jargon and industry-speak. As an example:

Just listening to your clients won't get you where you want to be. You must understand their problems before you can successfully provide an appropriate solution.

"Parametricism has supplanted Modernism's fetishisation of space with the supposedly more elastic, egalitarian notion of the field" (Patrik Schumacher, Zaha Hadid Architects). What is he saying? I have no idea—even though he is talking about architecture—and neither will the client. Jargon and industry-speak is not impressive; it is confusing. Be plainspoken and direct. Learn their industry's language. Use analogies that relate to them. Once you have established a common ground, you can then help them understand the nuances of your industry's language. This shows that you respect them.

Their Opinions Matter
Your client's opinions are significant. Make your client a member of the team. Realize that it is the client's project, not yours; therefore, do not refer to it as "my project." Too often, service providers overwhelm their clients. They are so busy telling them what to do that they forget to engage them and truly understand what the client needs.

In the end, whatever recommendations you make, your clients are the ones who have to live with them afterward. Seek as many ways as possible to bring their opinions into the conversation. You will find that some clients lack foresight. They request what they know and what gives them comfort. However, it is good to stretch your clients by sharing other possibilities, but if you overstretch, you may destroy your relationship (see Chapter 35, *Slow Business Growth*).

Great Expectations

While it is important to include your clients' opinions, it is also extremely important to manage expectations. In any service industry (and by human nature), the client will always want more for less. To make sure that the client is satisfied and that you can sustainably service them, you need to engage in a constant dialogue with them. You start with a baseline offer, then collaborate to find mutually beneficial ways to solve a problem. This way, you save yourself many headaches later on. Your client will respect you because you worked with them to find a viable solution. In the end, you respect them as well, as they demonstrated their ability to adapt and adjust their vision in light of the service you provided.

Return on Respect

Respect generates positive returns. When you solve a client's problem and you do it in a respectful way, you will be at the top of their list when they face their next challenge. Repeat business is the best possible return on respect. Clients can always surprise us. For instance, certain clients have stood out as potentially difficult and I thought I better avoid working with them—but come to find out, they have become great friends and solid clients. The reverse has also happened.

Become a Trusted Advisor

Take the Long View

Today's business world is in the grips of short-term thinking. Businesses try to squeeze their clients' wallets dry. The clients try to do the same to their consultants. Because no one leaves room for the long-term view, it is a breeding ground for cutting corners and making bad decisions.

Take the
long view.

The solution is to take the long view. Become a deep listener and consistently engage in a dialogue with your client that creates the space to generate value today, tomorrow, and into the future. If you do this, you will become their trusted advisor.

Choice Overload
Clients face choice overload. All day long, they are confronted with an overflowing docket of decisions. Some of these decisions are complex and involve significant financial commitments. Others are seemingly small. Take their decisions seriously, whether big or small. Help them find solutions, and you will establish the foundations of trust.

Deliver on the Promise
If a client engages you based on the solutions you proposed in your dialogue, make sure you deliver on the promise. Do not make excuses. You must find a way to deliver on your commitment. Yes, sometimes a client changes their mind and the scope of a project can take a new direction. If you engage in a deep dialogue with the client, the trust and space needed to collaboratively reach the finish line will be there. Value delivered is the bedrock of a sustained relationship.

Moving Forward
Once you have delivered on a project or product, the trusted advisor doesn't return to the beginning point. You understand your client and you should refuse to rest on your laurels. Listen and learn about the upcoming challenges for your client so you can prove helpful when the time comes to do another project together.

They Share You
The ultimate sign that you are a trusted advisor to your client is when they share you with others. The referral is an act of trust and an endorsement that you have proven your worth. Earn the right to be a trusted advisor and you will always have a thriving business.

Repeat Clients

Have a Relationship

There are three kinds of client relationships:

- One is with an individual with whom you have worked on a project.

- The second is a relationship with a company, where even if your main contact moves to another firm, you and the company remain engaged.

- The third is with a new potential client while you're building a relationship.

The unifying element is the nurturing of a lasting relationship. Great relationships can last decades.

Foundational Clients

When I look back at the start-up of our firm, I can see that we nurtured four main clients. A constant stream of referrals has flowed from these four clients. If you are running a start-up, invest your energies and attention on your early core clients. They will be your greatest champions and fuel for growth.

Spread the Word

If you consistently stretch yourself to deliver ever better work for them, your clients will spread the word by telling their friends and associates. These endorsements are better than any marketing effort you do to win over a new client.

Evolve Together

If you want a long-term relationship, then you and your client must evolve together. Our philosophy has been: "We don't just do projects, we build relationships." Careful listening, collaborative engagement, and commitment to bring fresh ideas feed this co-evolution.

Take a Look:

Work for Repeats

Relationships start in many ways. For me, one of my favorite ones started by someone kicking sand in my face. It was in the early days of our firm. I was taking a breather at the beach when the sand came flying. I looked up to see a friend's brother. He had heard I was an architect and asked if he could borrow a draftsman to help with his second store.

I told him that my business was actually doing projects, not lending employees, but to help out a friend, yes, he could borrow one of our staff. A few weeks later, he called back and asked to borrow a project manager. I sent one over to him. Shortly thereafter, he realized he needed us to get his second store completed. He was grateful for my help. Today, we have designed more than 3,000 stores for this friend, Don Fisher. The name of his store: The Gap.

The format and look have changed over the years, but the trust, commitment, and collaboration established in the first days have only grown stronger over the past 50 years. I appreciate these friendships and long-term relationships.

People Value What They Pay For

Free Is the Enemy of Great

Learn how to charge for your services. Don't be afraid to charge for the value of the work you provide. When a client pays you for your services, they will value them. Don't be cheap—it will make them undervalue what they receive and will ultimately kill your organization. You will not be in business very long if you give away your expertise. I am a firm believer that free is the enemy of great.

Freebies Hurt Clients

In recent years, I've observed a terrible trend. Companies have begun to ask service providers to invest significant resources into generating options that they then may or may not consider. In other words, they are asking for free work by requesting that solutions accompany your proposals. They are picking your knowledge.

A similar trend shows up with the much-hyped unpaid design competitions. At first, this might seem like a good deal for the competition sponsors, who then get full-scale previews of options without taking on any financial risk (see Chapter 47, *Win Real Business*).

The issue is that the sponsors are taking big risks. People without the balance sheet to invest in high-risk pitches will not enter the competition. You take a risk because your ideas are not based on the usual collaboration between you and your potential client. By entering into the competition, you are just guessing what the client's problem might be.

Skin in the Game
The best situation is when both parties have a stake in the project. I think it is good business for companies to hire service firms to help them address their issues by exploring the possibilities together.

Companies pay much more attention to their problem and the solutions you are proposing when they have "skin in the game." If a company is unsure of what it wants, then you are faced with guessing what it needs.

Get Rid of the Guesswork

The probability is low that you can accurately guess what a company needs from even the best Request For Proposal. Get rid of the guesswork as soon as possible. Even if the client does not hire you to solve the problem, encourage them to engage in a detailed dialogue around the problem they wish to solve. If they are unwilling to do this, it is a clear sign of a difficult collaboration ahead—even if you win the contract. You want clients that are clear-minded, plainspoken, and co-invested with their service provider to find the best possible solution.

It's Like a Good Marriage

Good marriages are a commitment to figure things out together. They require solid communication, patience, and persistence. It starts during courtship. If a company is already trying—wittingly or unwittingly—to take advantage of you from the beginning, it will only end unhappily for everyone.

Start Right. Finish Right.

When a client commits to truly exploring the problem, they are more likely to find the right match and get off to a good start. And by starting out the right way, they stand the greatest chance of finishing well—which means value is created, everyone can earn a living— and the process can begin again when a new problem emerges that requires a helpful service provider.

Power of Design

The Power of Design

The Rise of Design Thinking

Professional services firms are in the business of thinking. Their products and services are packaged knowledge. If you are considering building a service firm or you are a leader in a larger organization, I encourage you to tap into the rising power of design. Be a design fanatic, whatever business you are in.

Design thinking differs from how most service professionals see the world. The majority of service professionals are paid to solve singular problems.

An attorney will draft a contract, an accountant will manage your bookkeeping, and an engineer will figure out a technical solution. You can sell anything with enthusiasm, chutzpah, and the sheer joy of the process. For real success, focus on new standards for the rest of your industry to follow. In other words, put so much distance between you and your competition that they stop trying to keep up.

Design thinking takes on problem-solving from another approach. It invests energy into finding the right question to explore. Think outside the norm. By finding the right question, designers have the greatest chance of producing the most value for their clients. First, define the problem, frame the problem, and then solve it.

Once the right challenge is selected, design thinking sets about creating products and services that incorporate both substance and style. This combination makes design thinking rise above the strictly analytical thinking that is widespread among service firms.

Design Transforms Storytelling

Good design transforms a simple product and service into a compelling story that clients buy into and build upon within their own communities. Good design pays attention to the small details—such as the font on

Powerful design thinking
integrates four main
themes on the Process
of Design:
Ethical Practice
Thoughtful Impact
Experiential Design
Excellence in Delivery

(see also next section, *Design Process*)

your business card and your workspace design—and knows that every touch point with the client drives the story forward.

Good design is not just for your clients; it is also important for your team. For years, our teams and I have produced rich data from observation and surveys that have shown how important design is to making people more productive and clients more successful.

Design Is Co-Created

The value produced by design is co-created. You, your team, and the client are all involved. Successful professionals understand this and factor it into their way of seeing the world. I encourage you, as an owner or leader within any type of professional services firm, to tap into the power of design. Apply the designer's mentality to all aspects of your business. Encourage your team members to explore the field, attend workshops, and integrate it into their area of expertise.

The more you build design into your way of thinking, the more value you will create for your clients, and the more potential you can unlock in your talent. This team effort will drive your ability to have a strong brand.

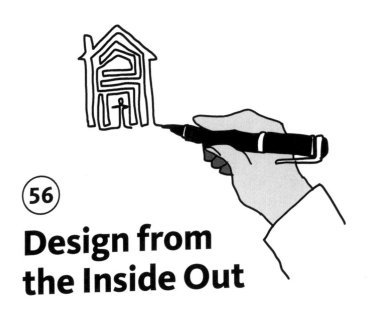

56

Design from the Inside Out

The first thing that most laypeople think about when the word "design" is mentioned is how something looks on the outside. In other words, they think about style and aesthetics. In fact, this is how most designers think about design as well. They are concerned about making a statement. While I appreciate style, I prefer to start with substance. I believe that design should be done from the inside out.

Inside View

An inside view concentrates on making sure things work and are easy to understand for the end users—an approach that applies to all service professions. Some professional services firms rely on complex language to make their point when delivering their work. From the outside, this is supposed to make them appear to be important. The challenge for the end user is that they have to live with whatever the service provider has generated. If it looks good, but the client is unable to understand it and implement it, the service provider has failed the client by approaching the problem from the outside in.

I learned early in my career that your clients are best served when you approach their problems from the other way around.

Take a Look:

Function over Form

Although my training was as a building architect, my first project was as the tenant development architect for a large, new office building in San Francisco. During this time, I learned a great deal about interiors.

Once I determined the relationships of the individuals working in the space, I was able to produce a responsible design layout. At this point, there were no aesthetics, just a functional layout.

Do the shapes and dimensions work for the types of occupants anticipated to be in the building? Does the building have the necessary systems to make it work? Based on this knowledge, developers and real estate specialists started asking me to look at the designs their architects were preparing.

I realized many of them had handsome buildings that did not work well for the people intended to occupy them. For many years thereafter, I was asked to review other designers' work because I was known as the person who took an inside-out view.

I did not change the architect's look, but instead rationalized the interiors of the buildings so they would work better for the occupiers of the space. Eventually, clients asked us to do the entire architectural design, both inside and out. Clients understood that by identifying the functional needs, you can work together to find the right solution.

I think this applies to all service sectors. If you solve a client's functional problems first, they will entrust you with other business problems. A solid example of function over form is the iPhone. It is a beautifully designed product, yet the real power of the product is its operating system and internal parts. Even though you cannot open the Apple iPhone, Steve Jobs insisted that the inside be as beautiful as the outside.

Design Must Solve the Problem of Opportunity

Remember this old adage?

I COULD
DO REALLY
GREAT WORK
IF ONLY I
DID NOT HAVE
A CLIENT.

This attitude stems from a widespread culture in the professional services community where the providers see clients as a means to achieving their personal goals and ambitions. They see their work as precious and untouchable. I suppose this perspective is okay if you are an artist, but it is no way to build a professional services firm. The proper way is to put your clients' needs first. Produce value for them. Then you can allocate your profits as you see fit.

You are in the business of solving your clients' problems. If you are good at your job, you will actually generate new opportunities for them. The key is to always concentrate on understanding your clients' needs, putting those first, and driving your team to open up new ways forward for the client. This makes you valuable and keeps you in business.

Take a Look:

Shades of Gray

A few years ago, I became friendly with Paul Otellini, the CEO and Chairman of Intel, the giant Silicon Valley computer chip manufacturer. While I was touring his facility, I commented that the offices were all gray and rather boring. Engineers, who apparently didn't think much about the environment of their employees, had always led the company. The walls were gray, the carpet was gray, the cubicle panels were gray, and the chair fabrics were gray. I teased him that color materials cost the same as gray ones. That started a conversation about the quality of the facility's environment. They invited Conan O'Brien, the late-night talk show host, as a motivational speaker, and he did a YouTube video on Intel's gray environment.

Paul realized that for no more money, he could have workspace for his team that was stimulating, encouraged collaboration, and showed the employees the company cared. It all started by suggesting they might add a little color to their offices. Since then, we have done most of their offices throughout the world. That is the power of design.

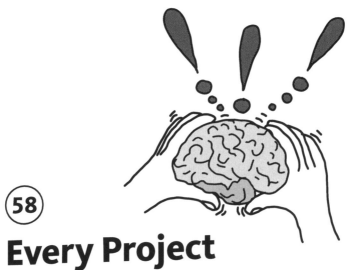

58

Every Project Deserves a Thoughtful Solution

Chasing Design Competitions

As I've said, the design community is filled with competitions. These competitions promise to bring visibility. The hope is that the recognition gained from winning will generate new business opportunities (see Chapter 47, *Win Real Business*).

While this can happen, I would not bet my business on it. When people chase design competitions, what they

Look for more than "look at me" projects.

really are chasing is an extremely small part of the marketplace; what we call signature or landmark projects.

Signature Projects
Signature projects give service professionals a chance to showcase their full range of abilities and creativity. Potential clients like these projects because they contribute to their brand building, and they feel it demonstrates their leadership. While signature projects are fun to work on, the world is not made up of only landmark projects. In fact, the vast majority of projects are not highly visible, and a landmark approach would not be the appropriate solution. These projects, however, deserve a thoughtful and creative solution as well.

Background Buildings
In my world, most architects are obsessed with designing showcase projects. These kinds of projects make the covers of magazines and win design awards. While designers think that creating incredible signature projects is exciting and rewarding, I am equally happy that we have built our business on delivering quality background buildings. When a unique signature design is appropriate, we are naturally excited to do that, too.

However, there are buildings in any city's skyline that fill in all the gaps between the flagship (what I think of as "look at me") buildings. Background buildings are just as important. Many more background buildings will be done than ever will be landmarks. While these projects might get less press, they do meet a real client's needs, and you build a track record. That positive track record, even on less visible projects, is what generates leads and repeat business. If you do enough of them, you will be invited to do bigger projects.

Thoughtful Solutions

Background projects deal with many kinds of constraints, including limited budgets, tight timeframes, and local regulations. For us, constraints are a positive influence because they drive us to be more creative and more thoughtful.

Boundaries push you to figure out how to create a solution that meets the client's needs. Determining solutions day after day is what produces truly rewarding work for your team. Whether the project is low or high profile, you want your team to respect and be committed to doing thoughtful work. They should always do their best regardless of the constraints they face. This is how you produce a culture of excellence. The good news is that the marketplace rewards excellence year after year with fresh business opportunities both big and small, and high or low profile.

Design Process

Make an Impact in Their World

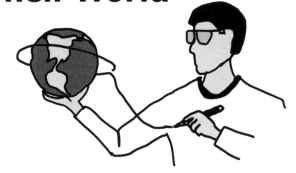

Always Be Client Driven

The design and professional services worlds are filled with small shops and big egos. These egos hinder providing great service to clients. I say ditch the ego. This is the first step in becoming a great professional services firm. Put the client's needs first.

You must listen, learn, and then commence the collaborative process. Understand your client's needs and business and what their issues and opportunities are. With this background, you can share your ideas. Always include the client in this process and dialogue.

High-Performance Design and Business Solutions

Many professionals attempt to dazzle potential clients with the bold approach rather than the value of the proposed solution. While the initial wow effect of the appearance or approach might attract a client, trouble lies ahead if the design solution fails to meet the day-to-day needs of the client. That is why I always encourage an inside-out approach. Work first from the needs, then the aesthetics.

Designing from the inside out ensures that you will make a serious, positive impact on their business. The more positive the impact you make, the deeper their trust in you will be, and the longer your relationship with that client will last as they grow and expand (see Chapter 56, *Design from the Inside Out*).

Expand Their Know-How

Size does not matter when it comes to expanding your client's know-how. Whether you are a single professional or a global firm, you need to contribute to your client's know-how. Work hard to share insight, information, and examples that can help your client expand their understanding of the kinds of positive impacts possible through your solutions. By exchanging stories and insights, you establish a running dialogue.

Engaging in dialogue is ultimately the best way to gain the deepest understanding of a prospective or current client. Such communication opens up layers of the organization and enables you to collaborate with the client in identifying their needs.

This is a two-way street. My clients have always been my best teachers. Clients also expand your world. Decade after decade, I've watched new industries emerge and old ones be reinvented. Each client opened up new possibilities and pushed me to expand my skills.

The dynamic, back-and-forth flow of insights and needs is what generates the kind of understanding required to make the best possible impact in your client's world. A happy client is the ultimate satisfaction a professional can experience.

(60)

Excellent Delivery

Bringing in business is one thing; winning repeat business is another. The key to loyal clients is to make sure you have excellent delivery of your services. This is a core part of the design process. From your opening conversations until the final handover to the client, you want to refine your delivery process. The best delivery integrates collaboration, execution, and deep resources.

Collaboration
Leading professional services firms have a collaborative culture. Start by integrating in-house capabilities, thus empowering you to make a richer offering to your clients. The next step is collaborating with your client to

find the right solution. Often I see service professionals failing to listen to their clients. They view themselves as the expert, and they expect their clients to take their advice wholesale. While you might have the better answer, you need to work together to explore the full range of options. Only then can you generate a solution that has strong buy-in.

Superb Execution

Ideas are good. Superb execution is better. Balance how you deliver your services, offer a superior level of technical excellence, and manage the constraints of time, budget, and scope. It is important that through the process of collaboration you develop mutually agreed-upon objectives. If circumstances change, make sure that you collaborate with the client to arrive at a fresh set of objectives. This clears the path for you to deliver on your promise.

Deep Resources

Make it easy for clients to tap into the resources of your firm. If you are a small organization, this might mean leveraging your professional network. If you are a larger firm, it means lining up your different disciplines so that they are readily available.

Take a Look:

Power of Design and Delivery

One of my favorite examples of the power of excellent delivery is my experience with the transportation company Union Pacific. They retained us to design a building for them. In fact, they wanted to have the tallest building in town. We met with them and engaged in a deep dialogue about their needs.

Coincidentally, another building under construction would be taller. This actually created a window of opportunity to approach the project from a different perspective.

When we looked at the actual size of their internal departments, we saw that the better approach would be to build a shorter building of 16 stories instead of 36 stories, and with a 50,000-square-foot versus a 25,000-square-foot floor plate.

This design would keep each department's teamwork flowing on a single floor rather than dividing it up among different floors in a tower. We added a central atrium so everybody was visible between floors.

At first the client thought we were crazy, but we convinced them that our design would meet the employees' needs, cost less, and be delivered ahead of schedule. They bought it, and now they have a special building tailored just for them. This project was collaborative, leveraged our deep resources, was superbly executed, yet totally different than originally expected.

Great Experience

Create Great Experiences

To create and lead a standout professional services firm, you need to master the power of creating great experiences. From the moment a potential client researches you to the close of a project, you should make it a great experience.

Great experiences are designed with three elements in mind: imagination, inspiration, and innovation. Experiential design thinking requires you to step out of your world and into your client's. By viewing the world through their lens, you can understand how these elements can be incorporated to create an enduring impact.

Imagination, Inspiration, and Innovation
Everything we experience is translated into some kind of story we share with others. If things go wrong, we warn others to avoid that experience. If you do great work, then your clients will have a positive feeling and begin to appreciate your brand.

Imagination is the key to producing exceptional experiences. It is the engine that gives you the ability to generate exciting stories. Getting people excited is one thing, but it is another to inspire them. Inspiration happens when you make a deep emotional connection with people. If you have crafted a truly compelling experience, clients will not only reward you with business, they will tell others about you, becoming your brand ambassadors.

The challenge is translating a concept into reality for your clients. This is where you will need to tap into innovation. It gives you the tools necessary to take the ordinary and transform it into the extraordinary.

Take a Look:

New Excitement
at the Airport

Going to the airport used to be exciting. The grand departure halls made you feel like you were off on an adventure or about to have a successful business trip. No more. Things have changed over the past few years. Electronic ticketing has reduced the amount of time spent in the departure hall.

Today, we dread going to the airport. Departure halls now translate into horror stories about long lines at security. Travelers hate arrivals just as much. You've just gotten off a long-haul flight, and now you have to fight your way through a maze of corridors that ultimately dump you into a dreary baggage claim area.

It is time for airports to reclaim their role as an exciting and inspiring part of life. The city of San Francisco agreed with us and enlisted our help to transform their airport experience. Our starting point is SFO T-3. The city of San Francisco understands the power of design to transform people's experiences. We are glad they entrusted us to collaborate in this transformation.

When we put ourselves in the position of the travelers, we realized that we needed to focus the story on an amazing arrival. Airports are the first touch point to a city, although most airport arrival experiences are terrible. By the time you get to your luggage or your ground transportation, you are exhausted. This is unacceptable.

We want travelers to be rejuvenated and excited about their new destination. The look, ambience, and services should say you have arrived at a great place. By breaking free of the traditional approach toward arrivals, we have revitalized the excitement and inspiration that accompanies travel.

SFO and United Airlines, Virgin America, and American Airlines are now the proud users of what has been voted the most desired airport boarding area in the world. It is an honor to collaborate with them. All food services are by local restaurants, not fast-food chains. Seating is everything from standard quality airport seating to swivel lounge chairs, and there are power plugs everywhere.

Ethical Practice

Ethical Culture

In our fast-paced world that too often focuses on short-term gains, you must create an ethical culture. Make it clear that you adhere to the highest standards. This sends a message to employees, clients, and members of the community that you want a long-term relationship with them.

Do It Right Every Time

Like trust, ethics is dependent on your every action. You cannot be ethical *most* of the time; only *all* of the time is acceptable, and it must be built into everything that you do. Opportunities always crop up to look the other way, take a shortcut, or tell a little white lie. Following that path is never-ending. Often the rules and some of the laws you must adhere to seem ridiculous and interfere with your goals. However, if you take an unethical shortcut, it will haunt you into the future.

Many times I had the opportunity to pass on or act on confidential information. I realized that any short-term gain was not worth the long-term consequences. It is especially difficult in foreign countries where the customs and rules are different. The Foreign Corrupt Practices Act makes payment to public officials cause for large fines by the US Government. Unfortunately, in many countries, it is the norm of conducting business.

Home and Abroad
Some cultures are poisoned by corruption. Stick to your standards. Do not ever lower them. As they say, it is a slippery slope and puts everyone at risk. If you find yourself with a client that is asking you to bend your ethics, move on. If you find a person or team inside your firm who is willing to go along with this rogue behavior, get rid of them. Unethical behavior can permanently damage your brand and undo all the hard work you put into building a great professional services firm.

Be Sustainable

As a professional services provider, you have the ability to impact the direction your clients take. Make sure that your firm is known for delivering advice that considers your clients' needs for the long haul, as well as meets their near-term obligations. Build sustainability, or long-term systems thinking, into your processes. This applies to accounting systems, legal contracts, design services, and all other professional services firm offerings.

Community Commitment

Invest in where you work and live. As professional services providers, we often work remotely in our clients' hometowns or another location away from our office. It is important that the advice you give takes into consideration your clients' communities. When you leave, they will have to live with the decisions you recommended. You can make a positive and enduring impact via your clients. At home, I encourage our teams to participate in their own communities. Get involved in civic organizations, your children's school, and struggling parts of the community.

True to Your Team

As an owner, be true to your team. Do what you say you will do. When you promise a prospective employee that they will receive a bonus, you must pay it if they meet the agreed-upon conditions. If you do not deliver, not only do you show yourself as unethical, but you also lose their trust. Even if you personally do not receive a bonus, meet the commitment you made to them.

Make a Difference

As an owner or leader, you have the power to inspire your people. I have always had a relentless passion for making a difference, big or small. Lead by example and always encourage your teams to do their best. The positive impact will follow.

History of Gensler

I have written this history of the Gensler firm to give you a better understanding of my experience over the last 50 years and how the principles described here helped build it.

In 1965, with $200 in the bank, we opened an official office in the back of another architect's office on Clay Street in downtown San Francisco. The architect was Henry Hill, a visiting professor when I attended Cornell, who encouraged me to move to California. Our drafting stations were hollow-core doors on top of two sawhorses. My first major purchase was parallel rulers to replace the T-square we were using. Jim Follett, a young draftsman, joined me the first day. My wife, Drue, who had worked in another architect's office, was our part-time secretary, accountant, and office manager. Our first assignment was interior space planning to help market the Alcoa Office Building.

After a few months, Hal Edelstein, my former boss when I worked in Jamaica and who was now in Florida, called to say he heard I had started a firm. He was looking for a change and wanted to come join me in San Francisco. A few weeks and 3,000 miles later, he arrived at our house in a Nash Rambler with a U-Haul trailer in tow. Hal ultimately became the chief architect of the firm.

Charlie Kridler was another early arrival. He was an all-around talented architect. At one stretch he left the firm to go teach in architectural schools in San Luis Obispo, California, and Washington State. An example of a "boomerang" (see Chapter 25, *Boomerang*), he returned and eventually headed up our firm's retail practice.

Putting the Firm on the Map

In the early years, we provided space tenant planning and interior design services. After one beautiful home, a Frank Lloyd Wright–style house, I decided that we would not do custom houses. We have done only four in the firm's entire history, and one was for a friend whose home burned to the ground.

A client we encouraged to go into the Alcoa Building had to move from his current space before that building was ready. We worked with him and found space in an old mattress factory. As a part of that site, the developer, Gerson Bakar, was building a very large multi-family housing project, the Northpoint Apartments. Gerson knew apartments, but didn't know much about office development. He trusted me to assist in the negotiations for that lease. The project turned out well and began our 45+ years of working together.

Among the many projects we did together were the first offices for MasterCard; the TV station for KGO; the planning and design of all the interiors, two buildings, and a computer center for Levi's Plaza; and a 1,200-unit apartment project in Newport Beach, California.

As we were finishing the successful leasing program for the Alcoa Building, Tony Peters—then Vice-Chairman of Cushman & Wakefield, the preeminent real estate brokerage firm—gave me a call. Bank of America had hired him as program manager for its new San Francisco headquarters. The building was to have two million square feet of office space with one-half occupied by the bank and the balance by other tenants. We were successful in obtaining that assignment to support the tenant-leasing program.

In hindsight, that project undoubtedly put the firm on the map. Not only was the building very significant, but the tenants who went into the building were the tops in their fields: investment bankers, management consultants, and many prominent law firms and other well-known organizations. We continued to build our relationship with Bank of America, the impressive list of tenants, and Cushman & Wakefield. Today many of these organizations are still our clients, including Bank of America, after more than 45 years.

Early Steps Toward Growth
Three years after we started, we employed about 30 people. It was then that I realized I needed to learn how to run a business. About 10 of us possessed leadership potential. I decided to take a night class in business management at the University of California Extension Program. Three weeks of classroom lectures told me that I needed to learn the material faster and I needed to share it with our team. Subsequently, we hired the professor, Glen Strasburg, as a consultant to work with us, teaching us everything from how to develop a budget and read a financial statement to how to interview potential employees. Glen ultimately became an outstanding consultant to us and to the architectural profession.

Meeting and working with the Cushman & Wakefield people opened many doors. Tony Peters got us an interview for the interiors of the Bank of Denver, a project we won. Jim Follett, my first employee, opened an office in Denver to do that assignment. We took a three-year lease (the length of the project assignment) and my agreement with him was to do a top-notch job for the bank, but at the same time look for future opportunities in the Colorado area. Jim successfully did both.

Finding the Right Team
At about the same time, I received a call I will never forget. On a Friday afternoon, a gentleman named Leroy Paris called asking if I did projects other than bank interiors. He had seen our name in a Cushman & Wakefield brochure. When I said yes, he said, "I'm calling from Pennzoil Oil Company and we need somebody to do a 600,000-square-foot interior headquarters in Houston, Texas." He then added a footnote I have always loved. "We are more than a yellow oil can. We are a natural resources company."

For a 600,000-square-foot assignment, I would have gone anywhere. We landed that assignment and opened a Houston office. People in the office panicked when I came up to them, put an arm around their shoulder, and asked, "How would you like to move to Houston?" They said yes, and off Tony Harbour went to Houston. He quickly relocated with his wife, but needed an interior design partner to complement his skills. In a serendipitous lunch with a furniture dealer, we discussed various people in the marketplace.

The furniture dealer knew a woman whose job was interiors for the bank in the Bank of America building. Her firm had passed her over for partner because it didn't have non-architect partners. I moved quickly, hired Margo Grant, and she, too, moved to Houston. Later she opened the New York office, assisted in opening the D.C. and London offices, and became the firm's vice-chairman.

I attended a planning committee meeting in my hometown of Tiburon, California, and observed a young architect, Ed Friedrichs, pitch a house he had designed for an unbuildable lot. To my amazement, he got it approved. After the meeting, I offered to take him out for a drink. He was a graduate of the University of Pennsylvania School of Architecture, but times were tough and he was working for a custom homebuilder. I hired him to work with me in San Francisco.

Discovering the Rule of Two
Cushman & Wakefield in Los Angeles hired us to do tenant development for the new Bank of America/ARCO Towers. C&W decided we should start a subsidiary firm called "Group Three," made up of people from a New York City firm, JFN; an L.A. firm, Selje, Bond and Stewart; and Gensler, with us managing the operation. The new firm never worked well, but we got the project done, and at the same time we met and made many friends. One group in particular, Ketchum, Peck and Tooley, project managers, liked us and encouraged us to open an office in Los Angeles. They also insisted we hire an architect named Marvin Taff. This was the first time we had opened an office that was not led by a Gensler person. Although Marvin did a terrific job and stayed with us until his retirement, it became clear to Ed Friedrichs, who had been commuting back and forth from Los Angeles to San Francisco, that the L.A. office would not become successful unless a Gensler-experienced person headed it. Ed Friedrichs agreed to relocate to Los Angeles.

About then, we started to realize that the "rule of two" was important. It was difficult for one person to do the management, meet clients, and do design. We realized that two people working closely together and in tandem would represent the firm better. By then, we had Margo and Tony in Houston, Ed and Marvin in Los Angeles, and Don Kennedy and me in San Francisco.

Getting Close to Clients
When the people at Mobil Oil saw the Pennzoil project, they asked us to come to New York City for an interview. I can remember that day clearly as Margo and I met with their project manager and the company chairman. In those days, chairmen met with interior architects regularly. After we made our pitch, they said they would let us know later in the day if we were selected.

Margo and I looked at each other and wondered...what should we do? The only idea we came up with: see the Rockettes at Radio City Music Hall. While there, every hour I would duck into the men's room and call them on the pay phone. (No cell phones then.) They would say, "No decision, call back in one hour." More high-kicking Rockettes, and then a movie. Finally, after two more calls, they told me we were selected to work on a new corporate headquarters in the Washington, D.C., area.

We assumed they would want us to set up an office in D.C., but surprisingly, they preferred New York City. I returned to San Francisco, and Margo moved to New York. Shortly thereafter, we received a call from a multinational investment bank to tell us the firm they had chosen turned out to be too busy, but suggested they call us. I surmised the firm recommended us because they didn't care to throw business to their traditional competition. The investment bank wanted us to do the interiors for their new corporate headquarters. Jim Follett relocated from Denver to help Margo in New York.

The Boomerang Program
About five years after the firm was founded, we hired Walter Hunt, a talented architectural designer and potential leader. A few years later, he took a leave of absence to run an exhibit design and manufacturing firm for a friend who wanted to take a sabbatical. Upon Walter's return, I asked him to move from San Francisco to Denver to fill the leadership position vacated by Jim's relocation to NYC. That's when we started

our boomerang program—welcoming back key people who had left the firm and returned. It is now a key part of the firm's culture. Ultimately, Walter relocated to New York to fill Jim's role in supporting Margo and became co-managing director of the New York office. After Margo retired, Walter became vice-chairman of the firm.

Clients Bring Opportunities

Early in the firm's development, I hired Orlando Diaz Azcuy, a brilliant interior designer. He worked out of the San Francisco office, but led the design of many key interior projects across the country. Orlando set a standard of design that the firm still follows. He later left to start his own firm, becoming a successful furniture designer and internationally respected, high-end residential designer.

Our New York office got a wonderful opportunity to do the offices of Covington & Burling, a prestigious law firm in Washington, D.C. We started servicing that client out of New York City, but finally realized that we needed to open a D.C. office to better serve them, and for other opportunities after that. Chris Murray moved from the New York office to Washington, D.C. Ultimately, Diane Hoskins—who had joined the firm in New York, then moved to L.A. and finally back to Washington, D.C.—became head of that office.

Note that we opened each of the offices when winning a major assignment in that community. We have used that principle each time we expanded. When a multinational investment bank asked us to help them interview locals for the international headquarters they were building in London, Margo went there to participate in the interviews. After interviews with a number of local British firms, the investment bank asked, "Why don't you open an office in London and do the project?" Margo headed off with a number of Gensler New York people to start and build that office. We initially transferred about 16 people from the US to help build that office, and ultimately hired many talented local people.

A Constant Hunt for Talent

We learned that the balance between experienced Gensler people and locals who know the country and the local customs was an advantage. Tony Harbour, a UK native, decided to leave Houston and return home to help lead the office. He brought in Chris Johnson, another Brit, who eventually joined him in the leadership of the office. After Tony left Houston, we searched for the best person to run that office. We found Jim Furr, with a strong Houston following, who has led that office for many years, and established the Dallas and Austin offices as well.

Margo had hired a group of outstanding people in New York. Two, Joe Brancato and Robin Klehr Avia, stepped forward and became key leaders and managing principals in the New York City office, and ultimately in the firm. During this expansion, the first leadership team, subsequently forming the board, consisted of Tony Harbour, Margo Grant, Ed Friedrichs, my wife, our attorney, and me. The six of us led the firm for many years.

Ed Friedrichs, who became president of Gensler, decided we needed somebody with more financial and business experience to help build the operations group. Ed hired my son, David, who had been a business consultant and worked in finance after Dartmouth and the Stanford Business School.

As controller, David worked with Ed and headed up our administrative and support groups. David relocated to London to help lead the London office and our European expansion, and later returned to San Francisco where most of the operations people and I were based. Andy Cohen stepped in to run the Los Angeles office and took a very active role in enhancing the firm's design process. After making a commitment to our clients that we would service them wherever they needed us, we added new offices in response to their requests. By then, we had expanded from mostly interiors to full architectural services, and a number of other practice areas.

When Jim Follett returned to San Francisco, he needed a partner to run that office. We wanted to bring Dan Winey onboard, although he was content in Detroit. When he did decide to move out West, Dan landed at another firm. Eventually, we won him back, and he went from running the San Francisco office to heading up the Northwest region. Today, he runs Asia.

To China via Denver

We arrived in China in a circular way. For our Denver office, we hired a very talented young designer, Jun Xia, who had grown up in Shanghai. He lived through the Cultural Revolution in China, but finished his architectural training in Colorado. Jun started getting calls from his friends in Shanghai, who were now in its planning department. As the government was beginning to parcel out plots of land to develop, it needed an architect to do designs for the sites. The locals, who felt the Chinese designers were not producing what they wanted, hoped Jun could provide some exciting design solutions and recommended him.

Jun commuted back and forth to Shanghai, working with his team in Denver and trying to be responsive. Travel was expensive and wearing on him, and the speed of delivery required in China was (and still is) much faster than what is required in the US. Accordingly, Jun relocated to Shanghai, where he built an amazingly successful office. He now has, among many other projects under construction, the Shanghai Tower, the tallest building in China and the second tallest building in the world. He opened an office in Beijing and works in various other cities in the country.

Planning for the Future

When Margo, Tony, and Ed started to plan for retirement, it became apparent that we needed to take a hard look at leadership transition. Although I am getting older, I still can't imagine full retirement. We also realized that gradual transition was a much more appropriate way for us to move from one generation to the next. In the early years, we instituted a very successful stock distribution program for our principals, Profit Sharing and ESOP programs, and support of a 401(k) plan. These programs allow our people to be financially strong when they leave. It also became important to make the transition from one group to the next. Although we have no mandatory age for retirement, we encourage people to move forward into the next phase of their lives.

After much help from advisors and consultants, we established a six-person Executive Committee. The six work closely together with other rotating members of the Board and Management Committee to lead the firm and to expose additional people to the roles and duties of leadership.

As the group developed and experienced more daily running of the firm and pursued new and exciting opportunities, it became apparent to me that it was time to step down as chairman, but still work actively with a few of my longtime personal clients.

In 50 years, we have come a long way—from the original three-person firm to one that now employs 4,800 people in 46 offices in 14 countries, with an annual billing in 2014 of more than one billion dollars. I am proud of every person who has worked at Gensler. It has taken the broad talents and leadership of our "Constellation of Stars" to generate our success.

Most of our 46 offices were started by Gensler people and supported by local hires. In almost every case, we founded each office to support the needs of one of our global clients. Although we are called a design firm, it has been our commitment to go anywhere and do anything to meet our clients' needs that has strengthened our relationship with them and enabled us to be a true full-service provider.

Acknowledgments

Building the Gensler firm and writing this book would never have happened without the support and encouragement of my wife, Drue, during our 58 years of marriage. Her contributions to the founding of the firm in setting up many of our administrative and accounting systems, and her guidance—especially with the women on our staff— have truly been amazing. Not only that, but she was instrumental in raising our four sons, and giving support to their wives and our grandchildren.

Drue encouraged me to hire the best people, male or female, and acted as a strong role model for all of us. I always respected and admired her support. She was active in the early women's movement, a member of the Middlebury College Board of Trustees, and past Chairman of the Institute for the Education of Afghan Women.

I also want to recognize our four sons—David, Robert, Ken, and Doug— their wives, and our 10 grandchildren for making Drue's and my life so enjoyable and rewarding. It is a special honor to have the ongoing opportunity to work with our sons David and Doug. They make daily contributions to the firm and produce outstanding professional services for our clients.

Thank you to our first board members Margo Grant, Tony Harbour, and Ed Friedrichs, and to our current Executive Committee, Robin Klehr Avia, Joe Brancato, Dan Winey, Diane Hoskins, Andy Cohen, and David Gensler. I could not have written this book without their ideas and commitment to our firm.

My son David met Michael Lindenmayer in a tent in the desert in Saudi Arabia. David invited Michael to one of our meetings, and we hit it off immediately. When I mentioned I was considering writing a book, Michael suggested he might be able to help me. He worked to develop the format, adapted the text, and modified it into the format we chose.

Doug Wittnebel is a principal at Gensler. He provided the sketches that illustrate the chapters and sections. Mark Coleman, Gensler's Director of Communications, led the book design and production; working with the very talented designer, Ngoc Ngo. Sandy Baker acted as editor and publishing advisor of the final manuscript. I am grateful to the four people who read the first draft of this book and made many valuable comments and suggestions: Jim Edgar, Marty Manley, Ted Hall, and David Gensler. Many thanks also go to my assistant of 26 years, Belinda Presser; plus Denis Rice, our attorney, advisor, and board member from the beginning. And finally, to all the people at Gensler who make me proud every day, I give heartfelt thanks.

Index

The Authors

Arthur Gensler

Arthur Gensler is an architect and entrepreneur
who founded the Gensler design firm in 1965.
The business has thrived for 50 years, growing
from a three-person office to the largest design
firm in the world. Its success is based on a combination of exceptional design services, innovative
leadership, and team-oriented infrastructure.
An early advocate of social networking, Art
cultivated enduring relationships with a diverse
range of clients, including Bank of America, Gap,
and Cushman & Wakefield. A graduate of Cornell
University's College of Architecture, Art and
Planning, he has earned many honors, including
the Cornell Entrepreneur of the Year Award
in 1995, as well as Ernst & Young's Lifetime
Achievement Award. In 2000, Gensler received
the American Institute of Architects' "Firm of
the Year" award.

Michael TS Lindenmayer

Michael is an entrepreneur, educator, and writer. He thinks about the core business and design principles required to reach scale and make an impact. For the past 20 years, he has applied these to for-profit and not-for-profit ventures in the US, Europe, South Asia, and Latin America. He is an associate fellow at the University of Chicago's Booth Business School. He contributes to *Forbes* and is the co-author of *Charity and Philanthropy For Dummies*.

Together with Arthur Gensler, Michael co-founded an education platform that teaches the core concepts shared in *Art's Principles*. Learn more at www.artsprinciples.com.

41569907R00178

Made in the USA
Middletown, DE
17 March 2017